Advancing Co-Teaching Practices:
Strategies for Success

≫

Sonya Heineman Kunkel

Kunkel Consulting Services
Cromwell, CT
2012

Advance Co-Teaching Practices: Strategies for Success / Sonya Heineman Kunkel

-1st ed.

Includes index.

LCCN: 2012901374

ISBN-13: 978-1468010688

ISBN-10: 1468010689

**For additional materials, including the new co-teaching APP
for Android smart phones, as well as resources, coaching
or professional development opportunities,
contact Sonya Heineman Kunkel
www.KunkelConsultingServices.com**

This book is dedicated to Marc, my co-teaching partner for 30 years.

All my gratitude to God, my mentors, colleagues, students,
my parents and family.

A special thank you to my editor, Kristina.

Also much appreciation to Randy, Robb, Sarah,
and Julie for their contributions.

Table of Contents

*"Special Education is instruction that is **more** urgent, **more** intensive, m**ore** relentless, **more** precisely delivered, **more** highly structured and direct, and **more** carefully monitored for procedural fidelity and effects."*
(J.M. Kauffman)

Introduction

Hi, I'm Sonya Heineman Kunkel. As a teacher, instructional coach and administrator, I lead professional development courses to help teachers advance their co-teaching practices. This resource condenses the information from those seminars into a stand-alone text so that you can advance your co-teaching practices, whether you have attended the seminar or not.

Much of the information in this book is derived from my experience as a co-teacher. I give credit for my knowledge to my colleagues and my students. I have learned many worthwhile strategies, not only from my successful practices, but also as a result of reflecting on my mistakes.

Co-teaching is a developmental process. It is important to reflect on what works and what doesn't, and work collaboratively on refining our practice together.

Co-teaching involves two or more professionals, but can take on many forms. In elementary school, we might find three professionals: a general education teacher, a reading coach and a special education teacher working together. Sometimes, co-teaching can be the result of a lack of space. If there is no place to put another classroom, there might be 40 students in one class with two general education teachers together. I've seen a social studies and an English teacher sharing one group of students. It is also used as a mechanism for delivering IEP mandated instruction. There could be any number of combinations of co-teaching that may take place.

In our classrooms, we are all faced with the challenge of educating students who represent a wide range of academic and behavioral diversity. Co-teaching is an intense approach aimed at embedding specialized services into the standards-based classroom. This form of collaboration requires us to have a shared understanding of a collaborative process. Through a concerted approach to specific strategies and techniques, we can support our students' progress in the curriculum. There is a variety of research that supports co-teaching practices. I would encourage you to conduct your own action research. Also, periodically check my website for research updates.

www.KunkelConsultingServices.com

In the pages that follow, I'll be sharing my best strategies for differentiating in a co-teaching classroom, although you'll find that these strategies also work for non co-teaching classes. When I give you a strategy, try to think how you can customize the practice to make it work for you. Co-teaching is a very personalized experience.

As a dabbler in cooking, I have a variety of recipes for the co-taught classroom. When you see this symbol, I am providing you with extra tips to spice up your co-teaching partnership:

Piccante (spicy/hot) picks are teacher favorites.

We'll start by reviewing some of the basic concepts behind co-teaching. After mastering the fundamentals, you will have an opportunity to self-evaluate your co-teaching process using a simple tool, which is the co-teaching developmental rubric. It helps you determine where you are, and figure out how to get where you want to go.

Please join me in exploring possible options as we look to move beyond co-teaching basics.

What is Co-Teaching?

Co-teaching is an instructional delivery option of two or more educators or other certified staff that contract to **share instructional responsibility** for a **single group** of students. This is done primarily in **one classroom** or workspace for a specific content. The co-teachers share **mutual ownership, pooled resources and joint accountability** for the group of students, although each individual teacher's level of **participation may vary.**
Friend and Cooke

First, let's examine what this definition means.

Share instruction
- Both teachers share instruction for all students in the classroom.

Single Group
- Co-teaching involves teaching a single group of students.

One classroom
- Students remain in the same space and are not removed for any reason, except for IEP mandates. Teaching is differentiated to keep students in the classroom.

Mutual ownership
- Co-teachers take responsibility for all students. The language used never refers to "my students" or "the special education students," but to "our classroom."

Participation varies
- How and what teachers do and their roles are agreed upon through a comprehensive planning process.

> **Co-teaching is sharing mutual ownership, pooled resources, and joint accountability for a single group of students.**

Setting the Stage

Co-teaching is co-instruction.

Co-teaching, by definition, is an instructional responsibility. There is a notion in the field that co-teaching is a support model, but actually it is not about one teacher coming in and supporting another teacher. What I have seen in my action research is that support models (one teacher teaches, one supports) get you through the day, but you fall short on long-term instructional goals.

In 1983, I was a special education teacher using a support model in my first co-teaching assignment. I immediately recognized this wasn't going anywhere, I felt like I was in a lake, over my head, and that my job was to hold students up with their little noses peeking up so they could get a little oxygen. But every once in a while, I'd have to drop this student, so I could pick up that other student, and then I'd have to drop that student so I could catch my breath. I felt like I was drowning.

Once we shifted to an instructional model, positive changes occurred very quickly. According to the IDEA definition, special education is not a support, but an instructional activity. Our overriding concern is, "How do we target the students' individual needs?"

Recently, there was a case in Texas (Klein Independent School District v Hovem, (S.D. Tex. 09/27/10) where the parents of a student received a settlement amounting to two years of compensatory education. The student had a mild disability that was supported during the four years he was in high school. At the end of four years, his grades were A's and B's and he was accepted into college. However, his learning disability, which was in the area of literacy, had never been remediated. Helping him improve his literacy should have been the end goal, so that he could have participated fully in college, rather than requiring ongoing support.

This brings up a couple of points about the Least Restrictive Environment (LRE) provision of the Individuals with Disabilities Education Act (IDEA).

The IEP, or Individualized Education Program, has as one of its goals the assimilation of the student with a disability into general education settings. This includes teaching the student with an IEP how to concentrate in the same chaotic environment as children without disabilities. For example, when you remove a group of students to a quieter space down the hallway so that you can read to them, that is a support process that undermines the goal of teaching students how to develop the executive function skills they need to thrive in the kind of dynamic environment they will encounter when competing in the workplace.

Furthermore, when you make a unilateral decision to relocate a student with an IEP to a more restrictive environment, you may be in direct violation of the IEP.

"Response to intervention (RTI) strategies are tools that enable educators to target instructional interventions to children's areas of specific need..."
(source: **http://idea.ed.gov**)

RTI (response to intervention) is a general education process requiring educators to use data to target instruction. Special education is embedded as part of the RTI framework, which is all about general education and core instruction. If the students don't succeed in core instruction, then we have to ask how we can further target what they need. For additional information about RTI, see pages 7-8 and page 68.

An important point and concept in our co-teaching practices is that both teachers are responsible for all students. This is not a custody arrangement where one teacher teaches Monday, Wednesday and Friday, and the other teacher instructs Tuesday and Thursday. This is not a case of "my kids, your kids." They're all our children, and that's how we have to approach this process.

Recipes

Usage: Scheduling options

Co-teaching is scheduled a variety of ways. It may take place all day, part of a day, or just once a week. The key is to be consistent with instruction.

My experience has shown that scheduling co-teaching every other day does not work for the students. It is very difficult to plan smoothly for an every other day schedule. I have seen good co-teaching practices occur on three or four consecutive days, which gives both students and teachers a sense of continuity.

Shared Resources

A vital piece of the co-teaching puzzle is shared resources. Both teachers should have copies of the instructional materials, including the teacher version of textbooks, and both teachers should have access to specialized materials, as well as general materials.

When a special education teacher is told – as I was, in my first assignment right out of college – that the teacher's books "aren't for you. They're for the regular kids," the underlying message is that the SWD (students with disabilities) aren't honored, that the educational system doesn't value them.

Likewise, general education teachers should have access to modified materials for their special needs students. An IEP (Individualized Education Plan) is an education contract that outlines the student's program. Any teacher who has a student with an IEP in class has to provide accommodations and modifications. All teachers need to have access to these materials and they need a repository for this kind of information (see page 109). It is valuable not only for students with IEPs, but for any student with discrepant academic needs.

Ultimately, co-teaching is not about modifications and accommodations. Those are the parameters, not the end goal. The end goal is instruction. Accommodations and modifications provide access to the curriculum and allow for students to demonstrate competency. Co-teaching is about designing instruction so students increase skills, become more independent, and learn at point of instruction while having their goals met through the general education curriculum.

The purpose of co-teaching is to create "specially designed instruction." (Kunkel)

The legal definition of special education is specially designed instruction, not specially designed materials. This is where the misunderstanding about the nature of modification often occurs. Modification is about specially designing the materials. Co-teaching is about specially designing the instruction; and it says in the law that we design instruction around content, methodology, or delivery of instruction. That's where co-teaching gets its legal weight. It's about how we deliver the content differently, not how we slow down the curriculum. What's interesting is that specially designed instruction by its very definition has some similarities to RTI (Response To Intervention).

Included in the definition of **special education** in Part B regulations at 34 CFR 300.39(b)(3):

> "**Specially designed instruction** means adapting, as appropriate to the needs of an eligible **child** under Part B of the IDEA, **the content, methodology, or delivery of instruction to address the unique needs of the child that result from the child's disability and to ensure access of the child to the general curriculum**, so that the child can meet the educational standards within the jurisdiction of the public agency that apply to all children."

Multitiered Educational Systems / RTI

The tiered system of education was created as a way of improving academic and behavioral competencies. Essentially, tiers are a way of grouping students so that special needs can be addressed effectively and early, rather than waiting until the problem is entrenched and resistant to intervention. The number of students in each tier fluctuates according to how well they respond to interventions.

In order to be effective, the multitiered system depends on highly skilled and effective general and special education teachers, as well as other specialized personnel, who can successfully implement interventions.

Tier I is General Education, where approximately 85% of students receive effective core instruction in basic academic skills.

Tier II is directed at 10 to 15% of students at any given time. This level is characterized by more intense academic and behavioral interventions for small groups or individuals. After a Tier II intervention, progress is appraised to determine whether individual students should return to Tier I, move to Tier III, continue at the Tier II level, or whether the Tier II intervention should be modified.

Tier III is directed at 3 to 5% of students at any given time. The intervention is more intense and of longer duration than Tier II.

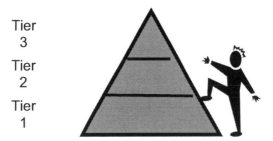

If it's implemented correctly through co-teaching, specially designed instruction can be a very powerful Tier I intervention in our RTI process. It's where we look at how students are doing with core instruction, how we flex our groups, and how we target instructions for students that need it. This is where we ask ourselves, "How do we group students, how do we teach our core, how do we differentiate our instruction?"

If we put it into the RTI framework, **co-teaching is a Tier I intervention**, because the practices focus on core instruction.

Here is a document that offers a more thorough explanation of
multitiered educational systems:
http://www2.tqsource.org/strategies/multitieredSystems/TQMultitiered.pdf

There are three main kinds of services that special education provides:

- **Accommodations**
- **Modifications**
- **Specially Designed Instruction**

Accommodations create access. That is not a requirement under the special education law. Accommodations actually fall under section 504 of the law, which is part of what we call general education law. Therefore, accommodations don't fall under the auspices of just the special education teacher, they fall under the job description of all teachers. Section 504 is the bigger law and special education is a subset of that law. So students with IEPs may be entitled to accommodations under IDEA, but both general and special education teachers can be held accountable to those accommodations (Doe v. Withers). Accommodations are minor adjustments to allow the child access to the standards based curriculum.

Modifications occur when we look at the standards and we start to sift or adjust the standards based on what it is a particular child may need to know. A modification is a major change in expectations. The child is not held accountable to the same set of standards.

Larry Ainsworth has written several books designed to help teachers implement mandatory educational standards. In his book "Power Standards," he helps educators create a subset of priorities derived from their state's academic content standards. Power Standards are organized by grade and subject, and they provide a safety net of knowledge that is critical for student success.

Power Standards are not geared toward service learning a little bit of everything, but rather picking and choosing some key core concepts and learning them deeply. Instead of focusing on the ten things defined in the standards, we may keep a student accountable to seven, because that is what he is capable of. It is better for a student to demonstrate competency in fewer key skills, rather than being exposed to numerous skills for which mastery does not occur. We always work from our Power Standards when questions of student competency arise.

So accommodations and modifications have to be implemented whether there is co-teaching in place or not. It is the specially designed instruction that is the goal of co-teaching.

Specially Designed Instruction
As a special education teacher, my job is to ensure a child's IEP goals are a constant instructional focus, rather than focusing solely on accommodations and modifications. For example, many students with disabilities have global reading comprehension issues. So as a special education teacher, I need to design instructional practice around reading comprehension skills that will not detract from, but can be embedded into, the curriculum on an on-going basis.

Understanding AMS

Accommodations, Modifications and Specially Designed Instruction

Accommodations Create Access

- Student is provided coaching from a teacher and given 3 warning opportunities prior to removal from class

- Student is provided a quiet, non-threatening, non-stimulating area to regain control when upset

- Science text is highlighted for the student

- Student given extra time to complete assignment

Modifications Change in Outcome or Expectations

- Student is given material that has <u>very different</u> expectations from the standards-based material

Specially Designed Instruction Provides specific instruction to meet the students unique needs. *The GOAL and PURPOSE of co-teaching is to provide Specially Designed Instruction.....*

Examples:

- Student is provided training in anger management, alternative behavior strategies, etc.

- Student is provided behavior contingency plan with student-selected reward and response cost

- Student is provided instruction on <u>how to</u> read texts for information

- Student is pre-taught science vocabulary/key concepts prior to the lesson

- Student learns a problem-solving strategy to solve word problems in math

- Student demonstrates independence in communication skills while the teacher employs a 'fade back' plan to increase student responsibility through an "I do it," "We do it," "You do it" sequence.

Case Study: Teaching Accommodations

I was co-teaching a mathematics class that was led by a phenomenal mathematics teacher who was very committed to her students.

Her process was to put a warm-up activity on the board. She intended for students to do the warm-up exercise, then she would teach them a new skill and give them guided practice. After the guided practice, she would ask, "Does anybody have any questions?" and the students would give her the deer in the headlights look. When she turned her back and picked up the eraser to clean the board, fifteen hands would raise, accompanied by cries of "What do we do? I don't get it!"

We found that the key was not to change what she taught but to change HOW she taught the lesson. We successfully deployed a technique called Chunky Changes. In Chunky Changes, you co-plan how you will divide the lesson into thirds. This removes problems that arise from information overload. It also uses the three rules of motivation: novelty, brevity, and variety. It varies from traditional practice, it's novel and it makes things very brief for the students. Students can digest the material without being visually overwhelmed. Chunky Changes is a Level 1 accommodation.

Chunky Changes – An Accommodation

Usage: Break down complicated tasks

Instead of teaching one large lesson, chunk the lesson into thirds.

Each third of the lesson may look like this:

- Mini warm up

- 10-minute mini lesson

- Assessment guided practice (2 questions)

Repeat for the next 2 chunks.

To spice up this strategy, see **www.KunkelConsultingServices.com** for photos of the accompanying guided practice folder and additional directions.

Areas of Expertise

Nobody is a content expert in everything. We all have our areas of expertise. If you're teaching a heterogeneous group, you may have students with disabilities represented at every level, from preschool ability all the way up to students capable of Transcendental Calculus. It's fairly safe to say that an expert in one of those subjects is probably not going to know much about the other.

In a co-teaching arrangement, it's important to honor the fact that two teachers are each being paid professional salaries. In these tough economic times, we have to be responsible with our economic resources and double the value of instruction coming out of the classroom. Otherwise, programs and teachers wind up on the chopping block.

How do we honor the fact that we have these two experts, and then design an instruction practice that creates good outcomes for students? The key is parity.

Parity

Parity is the ability to show your students that both adults are in charge of the classroom. The image to avoid is one teacher in charge, one teaching assistant. There needs to be an impression of equality, although equality does not mean 'the same.'

The unique perspective that each of us brings to the table should be honored as a gift. Simultaneously, there must be the understanding that each of us has our human flaws. That's where parity helps us. No two co-teachers will have the same experience, which is part of what makes the relationship wonderful. Still, there are guidelines to help you determine what that experience will be.

There are four kinds of parity you have to establish.

1. Physical Parity.
   If the special education teacher is always sitting in the little chair and tiptoeing around the classroom, what kind of message is that sending to the students with disabilities? If the adult teacher can't be included, then how will the children that teacher represents ever be included? Symbolically, they won't. Realize the importance of non-verbal communication and take that into account.

2. Logistical Parity
   Who handles what tasks? Should both teachers grade papers, or does one grade the papers and the other makes the parent phone calls? Just as in a good marriage, there can be division of labor and still there can be equality.

3. Instructional Parity
   How will roles be established? Who should teach what components of the lesson? What message are you sending by using singular language? In an ideal co-teaching arrangement, plural language sends the message "we" instead of "I."

4. Disciplinary Parity
   Do both teachers manage behavior problems? Do both teachers mutually enforce classroom rules and routines in a consistent fashion?

Teaching and Learning Style Inventories and Assessments

Before you begin your parity discussion, take a moment to explore your own teaching style through one of the free online style inventories listed below. Throughout your parity discussion, compare your style to your partner's style to help you establish roles, areas of comfort and a better understanding of how each of you contributes to the teaching process.

Also, you may want to assess your students' learning styles, using the information to discuss instructional opportunities and teaching assignments in your co-taught classes:

Teaching Styles Inventories

www.texascollaborative.org/TSI.htm

www.fcrcweb.ftr.indstate.edu/tstyles3.html

www.longleaf.net/teachingstyle.html

www.vudat.msu.edu/teach_styles/

Student Learning Style Inventories

Elementary
www.uu.edu/programs/tesl/elementaryschool/learningstylesinventory.htm

Middle school
www.scholastic.com/familymatters/parentguides/middleschool/quiz_learningstyles/index.htm

High school
www.learning-styles-online.com/inventory/

Other resources to Google
Co-teaching checklists, co-teaching roles, co-teaching agreements (between teachers)

My Top Parity Questions to Consider...
What are Your Top Questions?

Parity doesn't mean half of everything. It means that we discuss our roles and make decisions based on what's important for the students in front of us. What do we need to accomplish?

On page 15, you'll see twelve parity questions. Take a quick moment and review the questions. Ask yourself which questions are most relevant or most important to you.

My top three questions are # 2, 7 and 12. Your top questions may be different and that is because co-teaching is a very personal process. Here's why these three questions are important to me:

#2 – "When and how will we plan? Will we keep one plan book?"

The reason that's important to me is this: if co-teaching is supposed to be instructional, we cannot teach without planning our instruction. You can't singly teach without planning your instruction, and you certainly can't co-teach without co-planning your instruction.

#7 – "What bugs you the most?"

Because co-teaching requires an interpersonal relationship, it's important that we have conversations about the issues that bother us. This will prevent situations such as the proverbial straw that eventually breaks the camel's back, or the dreaded overly polite communication that stifles practice, such as:

"What do you think?"

"I don't know, what do you think?"

"Well, I don't want to tell you what to do, you're my colleague, that's not my job."

Don't be like Laurel and Hardy or the Disney chipmunks, who are so overly polite ("After you." "No, after you.") that they wind up trying to walk through the door at the same time and get tangled up to the point that neither of them can get through. That can be the result of not asserting your preferences to your co-teacher. If one teacher denies a hall pass to a student and the other teacher writes one out, that could be a source of conflict. Resentment can also build from a lack of trust or a disagreement about teaching methods. So think about what bugs you, and then talk about it.

#12 – "Will both teachers have adult size furniture in the room?

This question is not about a competition for the most comfortable chair, it's about the equal status that the furniture represents. Physical parity sends a non-verbal message of equality, not only regarding the teachers, but the students as well. If the support teacher is relegated to a student chair, how are the children who are represented by that teacher perceived?

Parity Questions

Here are some select questions to discuss with your co-teacher before you begin. Be sure and add your own questions as well.

1. How will we establish parity among ourselves and with our students?

2. When and how will we plan? Will we keep one plan book? *Google Doc*

3. How will roles be determined? How will we both work with all students?

4. What about grading, parent phone calls, IEP meetings, communications with guidance or administration?

5. What will we tell the students, parents, and other staff?

6. How will we handle various behaviors in the classroom?

7. What bugs you the most? *how are we going to communicate / disagree?*

8. What routines work best for you?

9. What do you like to do the best, your successes?

10. What tasks do you hate to do?

11. How will we set up the room?

12. Will both teachers have adult size furniture in the room?

Use the questions from the previous page as a conversation starter. Think about what questions are most important to you and why, and then have this conversation with your co-teacher. Many teachers who feel comfortable with each other skip this step. However, this step is the *essential foundation* for even the most experienced co-teachers.

Take a moment to look at the strategies on the next page for establishing parity. These techniques advance parity at the basic level in the co-teaching classroom.

The first two bullet points on the next page cover the simple steps of putting both names on class materials, on the board, and on the door of the classroom. I love it when I walk into a co-teaching classroom and instead of seeing "Mr. Smith," or "Mr. Smith and Visitor," I see "Mr. Smith and Mrs. Jones." It welcomes that teacher and it validates that teacher's presence.

Look at the fourth bullet, "Use plural language." The number one thing I listen for when I observe co-teaching sessions is the use of plural language. If I don't hear a "We" or an "Us," my concern is that it's a very unilateral co-teaching situation. "I expect you to…" or "I will be collecting your homework…" But the reality is, It's not an I, it's a We. And our language reveals a lot about how we internally think about our co-teaching.

The fifth bullet: "Share grading responsibility so that students see both teachers writing on their papers." It's important for students with disabilities to know that both co-teachers are involved with their progress. Maybe one teacher corrects a paper for accuracy and the other teacher provides written or elaborated feedback. That way, the students know they've gotten a thorough review.

Strategies for Establishing Parity

Creating Parity   **versus**   **Creating Disparity**

- Put both names on all classroom materials – this validates teachers' roles.

- Write both names on the board or on the door of the classroom – this welcomes students and establishes both teachers as equal partners.

- Have both teachers attend open house or parent conferences to create opportunities to connect with parents and answer their questions.

- Use plural language – words like "we" and "our" create common ownership of classroom and shared responsibility.

- Share grading responsibility so that students see both teachers writing on their papers – this shows students that they are accountable to both of you.

- Share responsibility for handling logistics such as attendance, parent phone calls, office referrals, giving permission for hallway passes

- Place both names on the report card and data team reports

- Take turns representing the class on data teams, child study teams and other problem solving teams such as Response to Intervention meetings.

- Understand your personal teaching styles (see page 13). Use this information to capitalize on your strengths and determine teaching roles.

- Establish roles – who does what, when.

- Create a "contract" or "agreement" with each other to avoid misunderstandings and create a terrific foundation for communication.

True collaborative partnerships are multi-faceted. Co-teaching must include not only the co-teaching pair, other professional partners and the students, but also the parents. One way in which to "enroll" parents in this partnership is to ensure they understand that both teachers combine their expertise to maximize learning opportunities. Every parent who has a child in your classroom, whether that student has a disability or not, should grasp the contribution each teacher is making to their child's education.

Dinner "Roles"

Usage: Establish parity with parents

Establish roles with parents by introducing yourselves.
Consider presenting yourselves like this: the general
education teacher is the "content expert,"
and the specialist is the
"strategic learning" or "strategies expert."

"

Co–Teaching : Advancing Practices

Advancing Practices

Case Study: Two Examples of Action Research

A Tale of Two Classes

I was co-teaching in a Spanish 1 class and we had a problem: in middle school, students with disabilities were being taught specialized reading, instead of receiving world language instruction.

By the time these students got to high school, they were behind in the curriculum, which was created with the assumption that students already had two years of world language under their belts. Since colleges are reticent to accept language waivers, students had to find a way to get through HS language classes and get credit needed for graduation; but they were already behind because we, the adults, had put them there.

There were two Spanish 1 classes running simultaneously. The first class consisted of 25 students receiving whole group instruction taught solely by the Teacher of the Year. I was co-teaching the second class and we were using advanced practices (Level 2, see page 21) about 80% to 90% of the time. We had 28 students, 26 of which either had 504 plans or IEPs.

By the end of the year in the co-taught class, we actually covered two more chapters at a faster rate than the single teacher. We credited our ability to cover more material to two things: 1) the use of differentiated instruction and 2) the use of small group instruction as our primary teaching method in the co-taught class.

On the same final exam, our co-taught students scored higher as a class average than the single teacher group.

Departmental Shift

I worked with a school's social studies department. The co-taught classes were taught as a whole group and only 28% of the students with disabilities were passing the high stakes test. We changed practices to limit whole group instruction to less than 30% of the time, and both teachers only taught in smaller groups (Level 2, see page 21). This was the result: we covered material in a much more in-depth way, there was much better discussion, more opportunities to respond, more time on task, and the kids actually learned the material. By year three of using Level 2 practices, 67% of the students with disabilities passed the high stakes test.

The social studies teacher declared that he never wanted to go back to whole group teaching and in fact, the entire social studies department decided that they were going to move all co-taught classrooms to Level 2 co-teaching practices.

So that is something to think about in terms of student outcome. We're not just doing this to support students. We're doing this to teach students and raise test scores.

Let's take a look at how we advance practices...

Two Levels of Co-teaching

We think of co-teaching as having two levels. Level 1 is typified by whole group instruction: both teachers are teaching to the whole group of students, or facilitating whole group instruction activities. Level 2 is typified by teacher-led direct instruction provided in small groups: each teacher is teaching to instructional objectives at the same time, using specific teaching methods. In order to advance our practices, we should limit our use of whole group instruction to 30% or less of our teaching time. Level 2 should comprise about 70% or more of our available instructional time. In co-teaching, our goal is to work with small, targeted groups.

Level 1 co-teaching options: (30%)
A process by which one teacher assumes the main teaching responsibility of the classroom and one teacher assumes a support role. Sometimes both teachers support instruction while students practice or work on cooperative independent tasks. (Kunkel)

Level 2 co-teaching options: (70%)
A specific value-added approach. Both teachers teach at the same time to smaller groups of students. Focus is on data based interventions, small group instruction, specific needs and skills as identified by the data, and specific IEP related instruction. (Kunkel)

Understanding Level 2

Level 2 is where we use differentiated practices, based on formative assessment of students. This is where we make decisions about:

- What students know
- What students need to know
- How we focus or laser in on what they need to know; and
- How we bring them up to speed.

Some of you are already incorporating Level 2 practices, and that's great. Some of you are just getting started on your basic foundation level, and that's where you start. It's important to grow your program at an appropriate speed, without biting off more than you can chew. Remember that this is a personal arrangement. You need to think, "Where can I start?" Even if it's just once a week for 15 minutes, you start there and you grow your program with the goal being to attain Level 2 for most of your instruction.

If you look at pages 22-25, you will see a rubric that I have designed with my colleague, Julie Giaccone, and action researched across many states. This rubric serves as a co-teaching self-assessment tool and helps co-teachers reflect and develop co-teaching practices. It is important to note that this is a self-assessment rubric and not an evaluation rubric. To understand how to use the rubric, see page 26.

Three stage co-teaching developmental self-assessment rubric:
Advancing your co-teaching practice through eight instructional domains

Developed and action researched
by Sonya Heineman Kunkel and Julie Giaccone, 2009.

	Domain I Communication p. 31 *Entails the use of verbal skills, nonverbal skills, and social skills*	Domain II Physical Arrangement p.41 *Placement & arrangement of materials, students, and teachers*
Stage 1 Level 1 Co-Teaching	• Guarded communication • Communication styles may clash • Lack of openness • Some dissatisfaction may be apparent • "Overly polite" • Issues of concern are ignored or not addressed due to a fear of conflict • Have begun parity conversation	• Students with disabilities are seated together • Impression of separateness • Class is always in rows • Little ownership of materials or space by special educator • Special educator does not feel free to access or share materials; asks permission • Special educator brings own materials • Feeling of a classroom within a classroom • Special educator remains in a quiet location waiting for an opportunity to interact • Special educator usually sits by student with disabilities
Stage 2 Transition	• Increased openness • More interactive • Increased amount of communication • Beginning of give-and-take of ideas • Beginning signs of respect for differing communication styles • Use of plural language ("we") • Use of conflict mediator • Parity/roles have been established	• Special educator begins to move more freely throughout classroom • Evidence of shared space between professionals • Professionals begin to share materials • Special educator rarely takes center stage in classroom, especially during instruction • Class is predominantly in rows, desks are moved occasionally
Stage 3 Level 2 Co-Teaching	• Use of humor in communication • Modeling of EFFECTIVE communication styles for students including: effective ways to listen, communicate, problem solve, and negotiate • Use of non-verbal communication, including use of signals • Teachers can finish each other's sentences • Both teachers communicate freely • Use of mini conferences to adjust lessons – ongoing • Regularly check on communication and comfort during planning sessions	• Teachers are more fluid in their positioning in the classroom • Both teachers control/utilize space and are cognizant of each other's position in the room • Environmental strategies are used regularly • Teachers' fluid movement is unplanned and natural • Student desks are moved regularly for grouping purposes • Definite feeling of shared ownership of classroom and teachers' space

	Domain III **Instructional Presentation p.49** *Presentations of lessons and structuring of classroom activities*	Domain IV **Classroom Management p.65** *Rules and routines, consistent expectations, community and relationship building*
Stage 1 Level 1 Co-Teaching	• Teachers often present separate lessons, often with only one presentation made by one teacher • One teacher assumes role of "boss", "holding the chalk" while the other teacher assumes the role of the "helper" • Presentations tend to be "traditional" in nature	• Special educator assumes role of "behavior manager" so the general educator can 'teach' • Rules and routines have not been co-founded, one teacher's system is being utilized • Management strategies were not discussed or agreed upon, are done "on the fly" as needed
Stage 2 Transition	• Lesson structuring and presentation begins to be shared by both teachers • Both teachers direct some of the activities • Often the special educator offers mini-lessons or clarifies strategies • Presentations begin to vary in instructional style, learning style, and differentiated practices • "Chalk" passes freely between teachers	• Increased communication and mutual development of rules and routines • Favor tends to rest with group approaches to management and not with individual behavior plans • Grouping configurations are used occasionally, some kinesthetic activities are offered each unit
Stage 3 Level 2 Co-Teaching	• Both teachers comfortably participate in the presentation of the lesson, provide instruction, and structure the learning activities • Students address questions and discuss concerns with both teachers • Flexible small group instruction, such as station or parallel groups, are the predominant configurations used for instruction • Strategies, differentiated instruction, multiple intelligences, tiered lessons, and learning styles instruction are embedded throughout lesson regularly • IEP strategies are embedded as specially designed instruction in the general education classroom	• Both teachers are involved in developing and implementing a classroom management system • Individual behavior plans, use of contracts, tangible rewards and reinforcers, community-building and relationship building activities are common • *Positive Behavioral Supports* are evident on an ongoing basis • Proactive and communication strategies allow for / create a positive learning environment for all students • Teaching in flexible groups with the use of kinesthetic activities is the instructional norm on a daily basis • Small, flexible groups receive instruction in pragmatic, social and cooperative learning skills

	Domain V **Curriculum Familiarity and Differentiation p.85** *Presentations of lessons and structuring of classroom activities*	Domain VI **IEP Goals, Modifications and Specially Designed Instruction p.99** *Rules and routines, consistent expectations, community and relationship building*
Stage 1 Level 1 Co-Teaching	• Special educator is unfamiliar with the content or methodology used by general educator • Lack of curricular knowledge creates lack of confidence in both teachers • General educator feels reluctant to "hand over the chalk" to special educator • Special educator feels it's difficult to make suggestions for accommodations & modifications • Special educator and general educator do not exchange materials regularly or in a timely fashion	• Programs are driven by textbooks and standards • IEP goals are addressed elsewhere (not in the general education classroom) • Modifications & accommodations are restricted to only those students with IEP's • Modifications are perceived as "watering down" the curriculum • Special educator is viewed as "helper" in the classroom • There is little interaction between co-teachers regarding modifications to curriculum • General educators may not realize that some students require modifications to content and they are responsible for these modifications too.
Stage 2 Transition	• Confidence with curriculum grows • General educator is more willing to modify the curriculum or accept modifications from special educator • Both teachers share accommodation and modification responsibilities	• General educator accepts accommodations, but prefers not to modify • The lesson in the co-taught classroom mirrors the same routine and instructional procedure as the other general education class • Differentiated instruction is used occasionally • Learning strategies are added in occasionally
Stage 3 Level 2 Co-Teaching	• Both teachers appreciate the specific curriculum competencies that each bring to the content area • All aspects of teaching are now jointly and comfortably shared • Demonstrated balance between curriculum and IEP objectives and needed strategies • Conversation and decisions have been made by the teachers regarding roles when curriculum familiarity is in question • Modifications are available to ANY student that needs them	• Both teachers are able to differentiate concepts that all students must know (big ideas) from concepts that most students should know (essential knowledge) • Accommodations for and modifications to content, activities, homework assignments, and tests become the comfortable norm for **all** students who require them- proactively planned • It is clear that both educators have planned accessible lessons and discussed exposure versus mastery of concepts for particular students. • IEP goals are embedded into lesson design • Learning styles regularly considered in lessons. Learning strategies are used regularly and are emphasized

	Domain VII Instructional Planning p.113 *Involves the on-the-spot, day-to-day, week-to-week, and unit-to-unit planning of coursework*	Domain VIII Assessment/Data/Progress Monitoring p.131 *Developing systems of evaluation, adjusting standards and expectations, maintaining course integrity, using data to improve learning conditions, opportunities*
Stage 1 Level 1 Co-Teaching	• Planning is rare and "on the fly" • Separate curricula do not parallel each other • The general educator teaches the group, the special educator assumes the role of helper. • The special educator works predominantly with students with disabilities • Only one teacher has a set of plans or materials • Level 1 co-teaching options are the norm	• Two separate grading systems, separately maintained • Sometimes one grading system exclusively managed by general educator • Measures for evaluation are objective and solely examine the student's knowledge of content
Stage 2 Transition	• There is more give and take in the planning process • Increase in time spent planning together • Plans are made explicating outline both teachers roles in the classroom (and paraprofessional roles are applicable) • Occasionally use Level 2 options over the course of the week	• Teachers begin to explore alternate assessment ideas • Teachers begin to discuss how to effectively capture the students' progress • More performance measures of assessment are being used • Data is collected by one co-teacher
Stage 3 Level 2 Co-Teaching	• Planning is now regular, ongoing and fully shared • Teachers continually planning, outside as well as during the instructional lesson • Teachers are able to comfortably change course during instruction to meet struggling learners' needs • Mutual planning/shared ideas are now the comfortable norm • Planning includes IEP goals and objectives being addressed through the curriculum • Level 2 co-teaching options are a regular part of the plan	• Both teachers use a variety of options for progress monitoring • Both are comfortable with grading procedure for all students • There is specific monitoring & use of both objective and subjective standards for grading • Both teachers develop IEP goals and objectives and ways to integrate co-teaching activities • Both teachers assess all students and are familiar with student performance in all situations • Both teachers names on the report card/assessment reporting • Collected data is analyzed, graphed and tracked for student progress. Data used to plan lessons, monitor progress • IEP data is collected, analyzed, discussed and reflected in flexible groups and class activities.

When we look at the basics for co-teaching, we're looking at the definition, parity, accommodations, modification, the specially designed instruction, and the two levels of co-teaching.

You'll notice that there are three stages to the rubric:

Stage 1: Level 1 co-teaching practices.
Stage 2: a transition between Level 1 and Level 2.
Stage 3: Level 2 co-teaching practices.

Self-assessment occurs across eight different domain areas. On the rubric, you'll see a page number next to each domain heading that cross-references the place in this book where you will find strategies for that domain.

Domain 1: Communication. The collaborative effort needed to communicate regarding adult roles and student needs.

Domain 2: Physical Arrangement. Once you and your partner are communicating well, you discuss how to physically arrange the classroom and how to move desks to get students into small groups. This will set the stage for very strong advanced practices.

Domain 3: Instructional Presentation. This domain helps co-teachers answer questions regarding instructional roles, such as: "How do we present? What are some new ways we can present co-teaching?"

Domain 4: Classroom Management. This refers not only to behavior management and positive behavior supports, but this domain also covers management tasks in the classroom.

Domain 5: Curriculum Familiarity. Co-teachers have conversations regarding curriculum knowledge, core standards and the impact of instructional studies. How familiar are both of you with the curriculum?

Domain 6: IEP Goals, Modifications and Specially Designed Instruction. Co-teachers understand requirements outlined in their students' IEPs. How familiar are both of you with the child's individual needs?

Domain 7: Instructional Planning. Planning conversations between co-teachers address issues such as roles, responsibilities, instruction and progress monitoring.

Domain 8: Assessment/Data/Progress Monitoring. Teachers examine data from assessments to monitor student progress, adjust instruction and target learning needs.

How to use the self-assessment rubric

For each of the eight domains, place yourself in Stage 1, 2, or 3. You may be doing a bang-up job in five areas, but perhaps you find there are three areas where you can advance your program. Your rubric scores may be at different stages in each domain area, for example: Level 1 in one domain and Level 3 in another--and that's fine. The question you have to ask yourself is, "Where do I want to focus? What makes sense for our co-teaching arrangement?" Go through the rubric and identify some areas where you and your partner would like to grow your program. Reflect on your students' needs, your curriculum, and your areas of strength.

Advancing Your Co-teaching Graphic Organizer

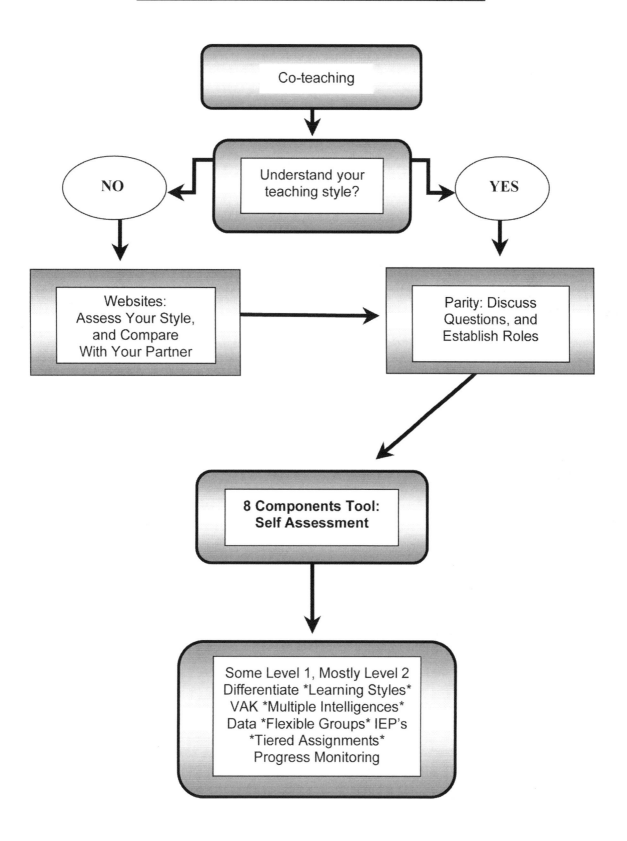

Palatable Portions

Usage: How to group students quickly

With "Palatable Portions," students are divided into manageable groups. Here are a few tips and tricks for separating kids into groups as efficiently and effectively as possible so that they can get down to task.

Color coding
Meet kids at the door with 3 x 5 cards in various colors. "If you get a yellow card, you sit by the counter. If you get a blue card, you sit by the windows."

Preset groups
This works if you have three or four designated areas for groupings that you routinely use. You type up the names for each group ahead of time, then post it on a projector or put it on an interactive whiteboard. The students see their name on Group A, B, C or D, and they take their places in the appropriate area.

Acrylic frames
The dollar store carries see-through acrylic frames, which allows you to post two pieces of information back-to-back. On one side, I have student names. On the other side, I have the directions for that group.

Management tip
I would suggest portioning the kids as soon as they walk in the door. If you allow them to take their places and then try to move them, it's much more time-consuming. Even if you're going to start with whole group instruction, that can be accomplished with the kids already seated in their groups.

Flexible Groups: The Hallmark of the Differentiated Co-taught Classroom:

- A critical management strategy

- Allows instructional match between students' needs and what students need to know, understand, and do.

- Groups have tailored learning activities based on students' needs and learning preferences

- Groups provide additional instruction or extend learning experiences to particular students based on data

Instructional Sequence of the Differentiated Classroom:

1. Locate or design a pretest format based on observed or anticipated differences

2. Pretest / Pre-assess

3. Lesson introduction

4. Initial teaching, Lesson and Closure

5. Analysis of pretest / pre-assessment results

6. Decision making and planning

7. Formation of flexible groups or choice activity

8. Differentiated teaching and learning activities, next class

Antipasto

Usage: Target instruction through Flexible Groups

Co-teaching relies on the use of Flexible Groups, which allow us to organize students in a variety of ways, based upon what our data reveals. These groupings are formed for all kinds of reasons:

• Tiered groups by ability.

    - Choral groups

    - Vote or rating groups

• Heterogeneous groupings by mixed ability:

    - Randomly chosen groups

    - Group by theme

Flexible Groups allow us to embed specially designed instruction so that kids get what they need as appropriate to the instruction of that class.

Caution: It is important to FLEX how you group students on a regular basis. Using ability-only groups can create stagnant groups in the classroom, undermining student motivation and success.

Advancing Your Use of Communication Skills for Co-Teaching

DOMAIN 1

Domain I

Communication and physical arrangement
lay the foundation for co-teaching.

Excellent communication is the cornerstone of good co-teaching practices. Co-teachers must make communication and collaboration a priority. Advanced co-teachers talk about personal communication styles, student needs, curriculum, roles, expertise, and teaching methods, and reflect on what works and what does not work for students.

There are three communication stages in co-teaching.

In Stage 1, the communication is guarded. Often, there are trust issues when a co-teacher is assigned to the classroom.

One co-teacher may reason:
"I think she's a spy."
"I think he's here to tell on me."
"By assigning me a co-teacher, I think my principal is telling me I'm not a good teacher."

Such fears make people tentative and reticent at the beginning of the relationship.

Stage 2 is characterized by professionally limited conversations. This is the stage where many people end up. You can be friendly with everyone you work with, but that doesn't mean you have to be best friends with all of them. Sometimes co-teachers keep their relationship at a very professional level, and that's fine.

In Stage 3, co-teachers often finish each other's sentences.

 "Could you go over and get--"
"Yeah, I'm on it."

"I was thinking yesterday—"
"Yeah, I already did that."

When you're on the same wavelength with your co-teacher, the communication is easy and you don't have to work at it. It's an ideal situation, but not everybody's going to get there, and that's okay.

The following chart is a self-assessment tool to advance your practices with interpersonal communication skills. As you look it over, you may find yourself saying, "We do all these things really well, but here's one area we can work on." Please make note that this chart is a reflective practice tool for your own private use. It is not intended to be used by others as a means to evaluate your performance.

**Assessment directions: Identify your co-teaching stages
and create ideas and plans to advance your practices.**

	Communication	
	Entails the use of verbal skills, nonverbal skills, and social skills	
Stage 1 Level 1	• Guarded communication • Communication styles may clash • Lack of openness • Some dissatisfaction may be apparent • "Overly polite" • Issues of concern are ignored or not addressed due to a fear of conflict • Have begun parity conversation	Ideas for Advancing Practice with Interpersonal Communication Skills
Stage 2 Transition	• Increased openness • More interactive • Increase in amount of communication • Beginning of give and take of ideas • Beginning signs of respect for differing communication styles • Use of "plural language" ("we") • Use of conflict mediator • Parity/roles have been established	
Stage 3 Level 2	• Use of humor in communication • Modeling of EFFECTIVE communication styles for students including: effective ways to listen, communicate, problem solve, and negotiate • Use of non-verbal communication, including use of signals • Teachers can finish each other's sentences • Both teachers communicate freely • Use of mini-conferences to adjust lessons--ongoing • Regularly check on communication and comfort during planning sessions	

**Condensed
Collaborations**

Usage: Communication check up

Here are some questions co-teachers should ask each other every four to six weeks to ensure communication remains positive and open. Discuss these with your co-teacher:

- How are we doing?

- What signals do we use to help us communicate non-verbally?

- How often do we approach each other during the lesson to debrief, adjust, or alter plans based on the needs of the students?

- How have we built in humor?

- How have we been using kinesthetic activities in the lessons?

- Are we modeling good communication between us during the class (do we speak freely between us?)

A sign of a successful co-teaching pair is the ability to make adjustments while teaching. The teaching pair can observe the students to see how well they're learning the material and then change course in order to better target instruction.

Does this dialogue sound familiar?

"So how do you think we're doing? Should we do something else?"

"Yeah, sure."

"What do you think we should do?"

"I don't know."

Or how about questions such as, "How can I help you teach the class?"

That's not collaboration, and it's not effective. Co-teachers need to bring ideas and strategies to the planning table. Both teachers should communicate their ownership of the classroom curriculum, students and instruction.

Communication Contributors

Timers. Since you have to time your groupings, some kind of timer is essential. You can get timers in all kinds of places, including on your cell phone, from the dollar store, and there are even free timers online, such as this one:

www.online-stopwatch.com

Signals. Over time, you will develop hand signals so that you can communicate non-verbally. This allows you to adjust your plan without giving students an excuse to be distracted. Your signals could be anything from, "Two more minutes, then we're going to wrap it up," to "Could you give me three more minutes of time, so I can finish?"

Condensed collaboration is adjusted instruction. Kids like to see their co-teachers conferring with each other. I see a lot of co-teachers that orbit around each other: "You teach the first ten minutes of the lesson, and I'll teach the second ten minutes of the lesson." That's more job sharing than it is co-teaching. It is important for teachers to have mini-conversations or sidebars during instruction to continually align and adjust instruction based on informal assessment of student progress.

Strategies for Creating Good Communication in Co-teaching

Sometimes co-teaching communication can be difficult. Use these questions to guide your co-teaching practice in a positive direction. Find time to reflect on your co-teaching by revisiting some of these questions on a monthly basis.

1. Establish your "Happiness Factor"
   - How do you feel about co-teaching?
   - Did you volunteer or were you assigned?
   - Are you okay with the idea of working with someone else in the classroom?
   - How do you feel about working with your co-teacher?

2. Establish your "Comfort"
   - How are you with sharing the authority in the classroom?
   - Are you okay with sharing space? A desk?
   - How do you feel about both of us using one plan book?
   - How do you feel about both of us grading all students?

3. Establish your "Expertise"
   - What do you really like to do in the classroom?
   - What are the most successful activities, lessons, units?
   - What are your expert areas?

4. Establish your "Fears"
   - What worries you the most?
   - What are you the most concerned with?
   - How do we handle our fears/concerns if this experience is not successful for us and/or the students?

Hot Sauce
Usage: Negotiate uncomfortable pairings

If your co-teaching situation is "uncomfortable" between the adults, students will often notice. Invite a trusted colleague to act as a mediator to help you with the above questions. An unbiased third party can be a helpful participant to establish communication parameters and to establish roles.

**Pizzicante Parle
(Spicy Talk)**

Usage: Model good communication
for students and establish roles

Activities can provide the means for communication in front of students. Many of them do not have good role models when it comes to communication. They may not have learned something as simple as how to talk to somebody and not be rude.

Co-teachers can model the language of respect:
"Do you mind if I take over right here?"
"No, go ahead."

When co-teachers plan privately, the key question to ask each other is not, "How can I help you?" Co-teaching is not support for the adults. We should not talk to each other in terms of assistance. Your questions need to use plural language and be more along the lines of "How will we teach our class together?"

That's your spicy talk, your Pizzacante Parle.

Case Study: Co-Teaching Conflict

Sometimes personalities and teaching styles clash. Some teachers resist the whole concept of co-teaching for various reasons, such as, "I have my routine, I don't want to change my routine," or "This is uncomfortable, I don't like sharing my space," or "I've been doing this for thirty years and I like lesson plans a certain way." Sometimes right from the outset, potential co-teachers are unhappy with the prospect of co-teaching and this can be difficult to overcome. I have mediated a few co-teaching divorces, and I once found myself in a dysfunctional pairing.

Four days into the school year and three minutes after the bell for class had rung, the principal pulled me aside and reassigned me out of necessity to work with a curmudgeon that we'll call Mr. Galoot. My principal told me, "I really need you to get into that classroom. He's got a large number of kids, there are students with disabilities, and some of them have complex behavior issues. It will be beneficial for all the students if we can find a way to co-teach this particular class." So I agreed and as I made my way to the classroom, I thought, "Well, I've got a lot of professional teaching experience, there must be something I can do in this class."

The first problem was that the principal had not notified Mr. Galoot of his plan. When I dropped in unannounced, the teacher looked at me like I'd blundered into the wrong room; when I told him I was co-teaching, he glared at me like an interloper. He gave me the wave off, which in non-verbal language means, "Go stand in the corner." I did as I was told, thinking that we needed to talk about our approach, but now was not the time. So I stood in the corner and reflected on my task. I felt like a college-educated flagpole. Just then, I heard the teacher say, "Students, pass your papers forward."

I thought, "Here's something I can do with my masters degree in education!" So I made myself useful and started collecting the papers around the classroom. Mr. Galoot stopped me and said, "Mrs. Kunkel, what do you think you're doing?" I replied, "I'm collecting papers." He replied, "That's not how I collect papers in MY classroom!" I didn't want to have a showdown, so I did the only thing I could think to do: I dropped the papers and left the room. I proceeded directly to the principal's office and told him what had happened.

We had our situation mediated by the principal. From our conversation, I got the impression the teacher really felt like I was there to spy on him. I certainly wasn't and that's not the role of a co-teacher. During the mediation, I made sure to employ a lot of "I feel" statements, such as "I feel frustrated when you embarrass me in front of the students because if you devalue my position, then you also devalue my students." He said, "You know, I never thought about it from that perspective. My impression was that you were disrupting how I collect papers. I was focused on the next thing that I was going to do, and I wasn't thinking about it from your perspective, and I apologize." We came to an agreement, though we never got past Stage 2 professional conversation. But this is where I really learned how to deal with conflict.

So I swallowed a little bit, he swallowed a little bit, and we apologized in front of the class. From that point forward, we made sure to demonstrate a united approach in front of students through our language and our actions.

More points to consider when co-teaching is uncomfortable between two teaching professionals:

What Can Cause Conflict Between Co-teachers?

- Differences in teaching styles
- Differences in philosophical approaches to teaching and learning
- Ethics and belief systems
- The feeling of insecurity
- The feeling that one party is a "spy," reporting to administrators
- Inability to work with others
- Issues of trust
- Issues of confidence in the other person's ability to perform well
- The use of terms like "my students" and "your students"
- Being organized versus disorganized

Strategies for Mediating Co-teaching Conflicts

- Ask someone to mediate (a colleague trusted by both parties)
- Make an agenda of what you want to discuss and share the agenda in advance with the other person
- Create resolutions and potential solutions
- Hear each person out fully and without emotion
- Compromise
- Use honesty and respect in your conversations
- Speak from the "I" point of view and not the "you" point of view
- Focus on each other's strength areas
- Clarify roles
- Revisit the parity questions in more detail
- Use an agenda to stay on task
- Agree to disagree on unimportant matters

1. Name it!
2. take turns w/ ("I feel" statements
3. agree on resolution
4. revisit in 2 wks.

Non-Traditional Ways to Communicate

- Face time

- E-mail

- Voice mail

- Digital recorder (musings)

- Shared communication notebook

- Recordings (computer, mini-camcorder)

- Shared blogs / Wiki spaces

Advancing Your Use of Physical Arrangement for Co-Teaching

DOMAIN 2

Domain II

Physical Arrangements

Co-teachers each need a teaching space in order to teach small groups. One co-teaching misunderstanding that tends to arise concerns groupings. In order to create appropriate teaching spaces, we start by examining our physical arrangement. How do you use the desks, walls, tables, counters, and materials? Where will teachers conduct lessons?

Co-teaching groups are structured very differently than cooperative learning groups. In cooperative learning groups, students are given a task and are expected to work independently as a group. The teachers "check in" with the groups as they work (Level 1). Co-teachers target instruction through direct instruction to the group for a set time period. In a well-organized co-teaching classroom, each teacher is working with a small group of students, teaching to a targeted instructional objective by mutual agreement after planning and examining data (Level 2). Arrange your space to allow this to occur for all students.

It is important to consider physical arrangement when co-teaching. Where will students sit? How will we design small instructional groups? Consider your classroom set up – how will you arrange the furniture to work in small groups?

Chefs' Corners

Usage: Create teaching spaces

When you're co-teaching, one way to establish parity is to survey your classroom and ask, 'Do we have two teachers' spaces?" If there is only one board in the classroom, or if there is just a technology projection unit in front of the classroom, teachers tend to think there is only one way to teach. You need to have two teachers' spaces for your Chefs' Corners in order to cook up some good co-teaching practices.

How can you set up a second co-teaching space? Here are a few techniques for you to try:

• Place a white board at the back of the classroom.

• Have one of the teachers sit and use a handheld white board.

• Create a roll-down chart. The way I do this is to laminate chart paper and tack it to a bulletin board along the top edge. When my laminated board is not in use, I roll it up and use a paper clip to keep it in place. When I need to use it, I pull it down like a shade and write on it with wet erase markers. I clean it with a damp cloth at the end of the session so it's ready for the next use. Then I roll it back up, leaving the bulletin board exposed.

Reflect on this domain and plan to advance your practice.

Assessment directions: Identify your co-teaching stages and create ideas and plans to advance your practices.

	Physical Arrangement *Placement and arrangement of materials, students and teachers*	
Stage 1 Level 1	• Students with disabilities are seated together • Impression of separateness • Class is always in rows • Little ownership of materials or space by special educator • Special educator does not feel free to access or share materials; asks permission • Special educator brings own materials • Feeling of a classroom within a classroom • Special educator remains in a quiet location waiting for an opportunity to interact • Special educator usually sits by students with disabilities	Ideas for Advancing Practice with Physical Arrangement
Stage 2 Transition	• Special educator begins to move more freely throughout classroom • Evidence of shared space between professionals • Professionals begin to share materials • Special educator rarely takes center stage in classroom, especially during instruction • Class is predominantly in rows, desks are moved occasionally • Students' seating arrangements become intentionally interspersed throughout classroom for whole group instructions • All students participate in cooperative groupings	
Stage 3 Level 2	• Teachers are more fluid in their positioning in the classroom • Both teachers control/utilize space and are cognizant of each other's position in the room. • Environmental strategies are used regularly • Teachers' fluid movement is unplanned and natural • Student desks are moved regularly for grouping purposes • Definite feeling of shared ownership of classroom and teachers' space	

**Delectable
Arrangements**

Usage: Moving furniture quickly

Space management has become a very important foundation skill in co-teaching. Every teacher knows that in order to manage your classroom and manage your instruction, you have to manage your space.

Draw pictures of various arrangements and post them in the room. Ask students to arrange desks quickly in order to have the physical space replicate the picture.

For teachers that share rooms: students may also be asked to return furniture to its original position at the end of class.

Level 2 Configurations

Two groups
It's much easier to co-teach if the teachers are on the outside of the groups facing each other. This is a vital management skill that you practice as co-teachers, to remain in eye contact with each other. That way, if the kids are misbehaving or off-task, you'll manage the behaviors as they are unfolding, before the situation gets out of hand.

So just remember that you always have your eyes on each other in the classroom and that you're facing your co-teacher and not facing away with your backs towards each other.

Three groups
If the desks are in rows and you're worried about moving them, one of the things you can do is to move them together so that they make a sort of a banquet table. One row can remain intact at the center to serve as an independent station. (see page 47) Teachers can sit at opposite ends of the banquet tables so that they can retain eye contact. At the end of the class, kids simply move their desks apart to restore the rows.

Rearranging furniture is sometimes not an option. For instance, lab tables can't be moved, but if the chairs aren't attached, the kids could simply move their chairs. Perhaps you could have a standing station: students come up to the white board where there is a task to do. Perhaps they have clipboards to use while standing. A simple way to make a clipboard is to attach a chip clip to a handheld white board.

Take a few moments to look at the diagrams and think about how you can arrange your space. Sometimes, it's easier to do this when you're in the classroom so that you can see what furniture you actually have. There may be a table in the corner that's covered in boxes (that, by the way, no one has looked at in 20 years). Maybe that's a table you can recover for your classroom. Take note of the movable elements (such as furniture) and the fixed elements (such as countertops). Perhaps the counters could be turned into workstations.

A Dash of Seasoning

Usage: Quick and quiet desk movements

I don't want to move furniture with a bad back, so I have my students move the desks. Left to their own devices, the kids might take all day to complete the task, but I want them to move desks at record speed, like Olympians.

They might start out a little pokey at first, but by the third or fourth time, they understand the goal. I have posters in the classroom that show different desk options and I put a sticky note on the one that I want for that day. When they enter the classroom, they see the sticky note, and they start arranging desks. That's one thing you can do to make it speedy. Another way to pick up the pace is to say, "See this configuration? I want it done in 30 seconds. Ready, set, go!" And you time them on a stopwatch. Occasionally when the timer runs out, I'll hear someone say, "32 seconds! Tomorrow let's try to make it in 30." Sometimes I announce that at the end of the week, the class with the fastest time gets a prize. It's amazing the effort they'll put forth if we turn it into a competition to be the winner.

I make it fun and I also work in some skills training at the same time. On high stakes tests, students with disabilities tend to have trouble with graphs -- so I find ways to post a graph of the Olympic desk movement, using various types of graphs. Students think I'm being silly, but they often consult their graphed scores to review their "Olympic" progress.

p.s. to make movements quiet, try putting felt or old tennis balls under furniture feet.

Physical Arrangement

Desk arrangements

Level 1 Co-teaching: Create space to ease movement
for teachers in the classroom

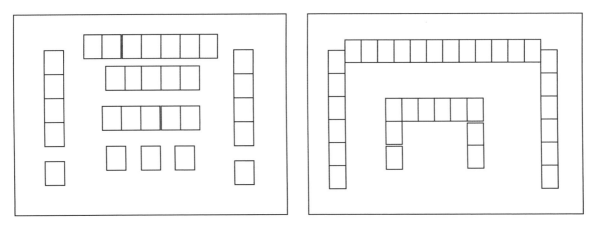

Create your own Level 1 desk arrangement style here

Physical Arrangement

Desk arrangements

Level 2 Co-teaching: Create space for students to move.
Shaded shapes indicate teachers' seats.

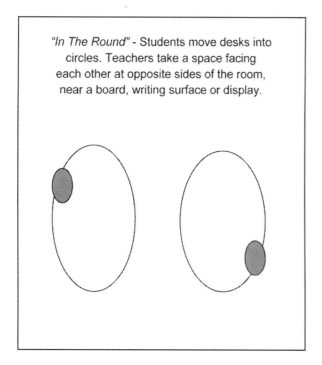

"In The Round" - Students move desks into circles. Teachers take a space facing each other at opposite sides of the room, near a board, writing surface or display.

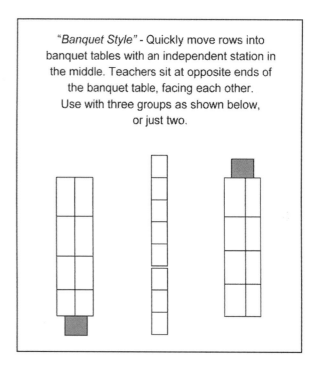

"Banquet Style" - Quickly move rows into banquet tables with an independent station in the middle. Teachers sit at opposite ends of the banquet table, facing each other. Use with three groups as shown below, or just two.

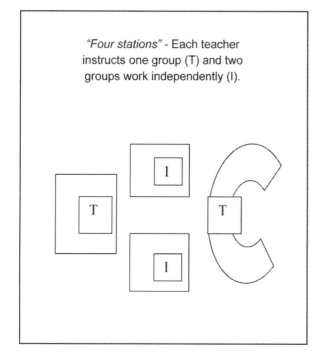

"Four stations" - Each teacher instructs one group (T) and two groups work independently (I).

Configure your own desk arrangements.

Case Study: Physical Arrangement

I was asked by a set of co-teachers to observe their 6th grade class and offer some suggestions for improvement. They were a new, young set and they had not had a lot of co-teaching experience. Their classroom had a challenging format because they had about thirty kids sitting at attached desks and chairs in a classroom that was shaped like a bowling alley--very long and skinny. The whole length of one wall was a white board, and they had hung the projection unit smack dab in the middle.

The special education teacher was in front of the classroom lecturing from behind a podium. I always have to smile when I see someone behind a podium, because it seems like it's being used as protection, like a force field. However, a special education teacher that lectures is not something to smile at because kids get lectured by everybody. The special education teacher should bring different pedagogy to the table. But that was what he was doing and he was young and he was learning. Since he was very open to ideas, I thought, "Well, we'll start from where he is."

The general education teacher was "drifting," walking up and down the desk rows. She was a very pretty, hip young lady, and she liked to wear very fashionable short skirts, and under the short skirts were these beautiful, shapely legs. When she walked by the students, they were more interested in her than in the lecture.

In the post-conference, the teachers requested, "We are looking forward to any ideas or suggestions that you have." We discussed the option of grouping students into two groups and they were very excited. We discussed how to move desks to increase student participation, time on task and teacher proximity. During our conversation, we examined how teacher drifting can be distracting to students. We also talked about how over-monitoring can create enabled behaviors in students who learn to wait for teacher help before independently engaging in tasks.

Advancing Your Use of Instructional Presentation for Co-Teaching

DOMAIN 3

Domain III

Instructional Presentation

It was important to cover communication and physical arrangements before tackling the question of how we teach. However, even if you haven't perfected those first two building blocks of co-teaching, it doesn't mean that you should wait to advance your instructional presentation practices. Instructional presentation is a look at how we structure our practices to determine co-teaching roles. There are many methods we can use to advance our practices in the area of presentation.

Often, I hear reasoning along these lines: "Well, this year we're going to work on our physical parity, and I'm just going to sit in the back of the classroom because I don't really know the students well, and next year we'll start co-teaching." The question is, "Can we wait for one year while students with learning needs do not get their IEP needs met?"

This is not an all-or-nothing proposition. You have to start somewhere. Start with something that makes sense, but you might have to grow in more than one area at the same time.

In instructional presentation, we have to make sure we have shared responsibility. We want to spend less than 30% of our time using Level 1 co-teaching practices and most of our teaching time (70% or more) needs to be spent using Level 2 configurations.

The strategies on the following pages will help co-teachers advance practices in instructional presentation.

With your co-teacher, take a moment to review and reflect on your instructional presentation.

Assessment directions: Identify your co-teaching stages and create ideas and plans to advance your practices.

	Instructional Presentation	
	Presentations of lessons and structuring of classroom activities	
Stage 1 Level 1	• Teachers often present separate lessons, often with only one presentation made by one teacher • One teacher assumes role of "boss", "holding the chalk" while the other teacher the role of the "helper" • Presentations tend to be "traditional" in nature	Ideas for Advancing Practices in Instructional Presentation
Stage 2 Transition	• Lesson structuring and presentation begins to be shared by both teachers • Both teachers direct some of the activities • Often the special educator offers mini-lessons or clarifies strategies • Presentations begin to vary in instructional style, learning styles, and differentiated practices • "Chalk" passes freely between teachers	
Stage 3 Level 2	• Both teachers comfortably participate in the presentation of the lesson, provide instruction, and structure the learning activities • Students address questions and discuss concerns with both teachers • Flexible small group instruction like station or parallel groups are the predominate configurations used for instruction • Strategies, differentiated instruction, multiple intelligences, tiered lessons, learning styles instruction embedded throughout lesson regularly • IEP strategies are embedded as specially designed instruction in the general education classroom	

Below are examples of the teaching methods for Level 1 and Level 2 practices.

Co-Teaching
"Sharing mutual ownership, pooled resources and joint accountability for a single group of students"

Level 1 Practices: (Whole Group Instruction) (30%)
- Speak and Add
- Speaker and Writer
- One Teach, One Facilitate
- One Teach, One Assess
- One Teach, One Take Data
- One Teach, One Support
- One Teach, One Handle Materials
- Two Facilitate (whole group)
- Turn Taking (teachers in front of the room together)
- Cooperative learning groups with one or two teacher facilitation

Level 2 Practices: (Small Flexible Groupings) (70%)
- Parallel or Mirror Lessons (same style)
- Parallel or Mirror Lessons (differentiated styles)
- Parallel or Mirror Lessons (learning styles)
- Two station Flip Flop
- Two station Pre-teach and Enrich
- Three station rotation
- Three stations, tiered
- Four station rotation
- Four stations with Flip/Flop
- Skills Groups
- Enrichment Groups
- Pre-teaching Groups
- Re-teaching Groups
- Assessment/Progress Monitoring Groups
- Six stations with interrupters

Important tips for setting up Level 2 practices
1. Agree on room arrangement
2. Plan materials
3. Include kinesthetic activities
4. Pre-determine switch times and which teacher will be in charge of "the clock."
5. Discuss management of independent groups.

Practices for Level 1 and Level 2

There are two kinds of groups: those that are teacher-led instructional groups and the cooperative learning groups, which have an independent task. Co-teaching at Level 2 consists of teacher-led groups wherein each teacher is instructing a smaller group of students focused on a data-derived instructional objective. Student needs for accommodations, modifications, and specially designed instruction are embedded into the small group lesson. At Level 1, teachers facilitate general whole group learning. At Level 2, the practices focus on specific instructional presentation in small groups.

Treat your co-teacher's different teaching style as an advantage rather than a conflict to be solved. It's important to be flexible in order to capitalize on the talents that each teacher brings to the table. One teacher may be more traditional in style. The other may be a free spirit. In differentiated instruction, there is room for multiple approaches.

Level 1 Practices

Speak and Add

Both teachers are at the front of the classroom. One person is speaking and the other person is adding in, clarifying key points in the lesson.

Speaker and Writer

One person speaks and the other person writes and records. This can be combined with the previous practice, which then becomes Speak and Add and Write.

One Teach, One Facilitate

One teacher teaches and the other teacher walks around the class checking on students.

This is my least favorite of all teaching configurations. It tends to be overused due to a lack of planning and a lack of clarity about what co-teaching is. A little bit of help during guided practice is all right. There is more we can do that will utilize teaching expertise for maximum student benefit.

You must be cautious with this approach, as it has major negative side effects over time.

> **CAUTION with Level 1**
>
> To use an analogy, when we facilitate over a child's shoulder, we give him a fish to eat for a day, rather than teaching him how to fish for a lifetime. The biggest problem here is one of dependence. Students who come through a system where they have been supported in co-teaching get so used to being helped and enabled that by the time they get to high school, they sit back, cross their arms, and you can read in their eyes, "Teach me, I dare you. Why should I listen to the teacher in the front of the classroom, when that walk-around teacher is going to come around with a pencil, write my name on my paper for me, and tell me what to do and how to do it? So instead of paying attention, let me find something else that's entertaining. I'm going to play video games in my head. I'm going to be an annoyance to the five people around me. Or maybe I'll just drive my teacher nuts to see how long it takes for her to blow her temper."

One Teach, One Assess

One teacher teaches, while one teacher assesses. For example, while one teacher is teaching, the other can pull three or four kids aside and give them a one-minute mini quiz on the top five questions that are going to be on the test, to see who knows them and who doesn't.

"What's the answer for this? What do you know about that?" You can check off whether the kids got three or five questions right, and then if they didn't know the answers, you have the key information to form small, flexible groups the next day so that you can pre teach them what they missed.

One Teach, One Support
One teacher teaches while the other supports students. Usually you see one teacher sitting down next to a student. This is a configuration that can create enabled student behaviors if it is overused.

Two Facilitate, Whole Group
This configuration is used during guided practice or during cooperative learning groups.

Turn Taking
One teacher teaches while the other teacher remains "dormant," then teachers switch roles. You have to be careful with this approach, as it can look like job sharing if done incorrectly.

> Tip: Level 1
> A facilitation of
> the teacher's role
>
> Keep a clipboard
> on which you take data:
> who responded,
> who understands it
> and who doesn't.
> This handy data
> will allow you to plan
> how to form
> your flexible groups.

Level 2 Practices

To describe some of these practices I waved my magic wand and created an imaginary co-teacher named Lenora, who is a terrific co-teacher. She communicates well and trusts me as her co-teacher. She has a positive outlook from which all students can learn. She is flexible and willing to do whatever it takes to ensure student achievement.

Parallel or Mirror Lessons (same style)

Say that Lenora and I are going to co-teach math and today we're teaching fractions.

We take our class of thirty students and we split them down the middle. We arrange the groups so that Lenora and I have eye contact. We can see what's going on with each other, and it helps us with pacing. We teach the exact same lesson the same way to two small groups of students (15 in each group).

See pages 62-64 for visuals that represent the following ideas:

Parallel or Mirror Lessons (differentiated styles)

For this practice, we still have our two groups, but now we're going to differentiate our teaching styles. Lenora's going to teach using one process and I'm going to teach focusing on a different process. We differentiated our processes, but we're still covering the same material.

Parallel or Mirror Lessons (learning styles)

We teach the same lesson, grouping students by learning style strengths. Lenora is going to lecture (auditory) and I'm going to create an activity (kinesthetic) for students to learn the same material to the same level of specificity.

2 Station Flip/Flop

In this example, Lenora and I are teaching two interrelated skills.
Lenora is teaching vocabulary and I'm teaching writing process.
After twenty minutes, we're going to flip flop – her students are going to come to me, and mine are going to go to her.

> Q&A – Parallel Lessons
>
> Q: What do you do with kids who are distracted by two teachers talking at the same time during parallel lessons?
>
> A: Say that Tommy Turnaround is with Lenora, but he's paying attention to my lesson. There are two options: either move Tommy to the group that attracts his interest, or leave him be and let him turn around to pay attention to the other (exact same) lesson. Either way, he ends up learning the lesson.

> For differentiation, you pre-assess your students and then you have two choices: you can either tier your activity or make it a choice activity. In this example, we have tiered it: Lenora got the kids that are ready for the skill and I teach the kids that need a little pre-teaching first.

Two Group Pre-Teach Enrich Switch

Let's say that Lenora and I have pre-assessed our students' ability to reduce common fractions.

- I am going to pre-teach the group that isn't quite ready for the lesson.
- Lenora, the content teacher, is going to teach the lesson on reducing fractions.

After twenty minutes, the groups are going to switch.

- My group goes to Lenora and she teaches the same lesson on reducing fractions to the second group that had received pre-teaching.
- Lenora's group comes to me and I either re-teach or enrich the group that received the content lesson first.

One group needed more information before entering into the lesson, and one group was able to get re-teaching, or go beyond the lesson.

3 Station Rotation

Two stations are teacher-taught, and there is an independent station. At a timed interval, the groups switch. For example: one group is learning key content with Lenora, one group is learning vocabulary with me, and the independent group is learning through a Pass the Problem activity (see page 58). After fifteen minutes, the kids rotate to the next station. The kids can be grouped by the criteria you consider most important.

What's nice about this configuration is that the opportunities to respond are doubled. In a whole group class, you ask a question, students raise their hands to answer, and you call on one student. Small group instruction is a way to increase opportunities to respond. We co-teach because we have certain students in the classroom who have trouble learning. In a large group, those kids don't always like to respond because they are embarrassed or unsure of their answers. In small groups, they are more likely to respond because it is safer and more intimate.

3 Station Tiers

Another option here is a tiered assignment, such as the Colorful Concoction strategy on page 60. Students are assigned to ability level groups. Students remain with their groups and teachers rotate to give groups mini-lessons.

4 Stations Mini-Lessons

There are two teacher-led stations where the students receive mini-lessons, and two independent stations. Students are equally divided into four groups and rotate based on a pre-determined timed fashion. For example, in a 40-minute lesson block, students would spend ten minutes at each of the four stations.

4 Station Flip/Flop

Each teacher is responsible for only two groups of students, for a total of four groups. Teacher one teaches his/her first group and then switches and teaches his/her second group. Teacher two does the same. This allows for a variety of focused skill development. For example, in a 40-minute lesson block, each teacher will see only two groups for 20 minutes each.

Skills Groups

These are small groups we put together based on specific criteria. Maybe you have reviewed test scores and you form groups to focus on specific items students missed. These are short-term quick groups.

You might work with four particular kids on one specific issue for five minutes, then return them to the mix and get four more kids. It's a way of targeting instruction that kids need. It could be the same skill for each group, or it could be individualized, based on kids who have different needs.

Enrichment Groups

Take opportunities for one teacher to work with students on extending or enriching the curriculum.

Re-teaching

Re-teach materials students did not master.
There are all kinds of re-teaching opportunities, which are needed to clarify or pinpoint instructional deficits and/or student needs.

Assessment-Progress Monitoring

Evaluate student competency with material by conducting mini-assessments. These can be oral or written opportunities.

Six Stations with Interrupters

Interrupters are mini teaching opportunities that help to clarify a point. They take less than two minutes and usually include videos or dramatic elements.

Think of interrupters as a commercial that occurs while students transition between stations. For a six-station configuration, I recommend they occur every other rotation. That is, interrupters will occur three times during the six rotations.

Try this practice for multi-faceted lessons. This configuration also works well for block schedules or multiple day lessons.

Instructions for this practice are on page 61.

Pre-teaching for Success

Pre-teach concepts or pre-teach the lesson. Kids arrive at the classroom and there's a "Do Now" activity on the board. But in any class, there are always about five fidgety kids that take two minutes to sit down, and another five minutes to find their pencils, and another four minutes to pick their heads up. By that time, they have successfully manipulated their way out of doing the warm-up activity. So I preemptively grab those five kids and I provide pre-teaching of the lesson. That way, when the whole group receives the lesson, the pre-taught kids can enter the lesson with confidence and experience success.

Pass the Problem

Usage: Small group constructive independent work – for Level 2 co-teaching

To help you envision how to advance co-teaching, here is a simple procedure that I call
Pass the Problem.

The best way to advance your co-teaching practices is to work in small groups.

Imagine a classroom with 30 children, divided into three groups. Teacher 1 will work with the first group
on vocabulary. Teacher 2 will work with the second group on some important academic area. And the
third group, the independent group, is going to participate in the Pass the Problem activity.

How to implement this strategy
For a group of 10 students, you will need:

10 white boards	1 two-minute egg timer
10 dry erase markers	3 x 5 index cards
10 dry erasers	10 related problems to solve
1 wet erase marker (the type used with overhead projectors, for example)	

How to set up Pass the Problem
If you were using this strategy for a math class, you would first devise 10 math problems that are similar
in nature or that practice the same skill, but in 10 different ways. You write the problem on the top half of
the white board with the wet erase marker. On the back of each board, you tape a 3 x 5 inch card with
the answer to the problem.

How to conduct Pass the Problem
The independent study group students are each given one board, a dry erase marker and an eraser.

The two-minute timer is set by one student to indicate to students to begin solving the problem on their
board. The students use the dry erase markers to practice the problem on the bottom half of the board.
At the end of two minutes, everyone turns their board over and takes half a minute or so to compare the
answer on the 3 x 5 card with their own solution to the problem. They correct their answers and when
they're done, they erase their work on the bottom of the boards. The original problem that was written
with the wet erase marker remains. The students pass the problem to the student sitting to their right and
the timer is reset.

By using the Pass the Problem strategy, students are engaged in important work that keeps them on task while other students receive targeted small group instruction from a teacher. The goal in co-teaching is to work with small, targeted groups.

In this particular example, it would take 25 to 30 minutes for the group to complete the exercise. It could be adjusted, depending on how much time you had. If you only had half the time, you might only devise 5 problems.

The independent group will be working at a rapid pace, which prevents students from going off task. The example given was for math problems, but it could be used for any number of disciplines. It would work very well with vocabulary or grammar exercises, for instance. So think about how you might adapt this strategy to your particular teaching challenge.

At the end of the session, you can clear the boards by washing away the wet erase marker with a damp cloth.

Where to find white board

In the construction department at your local building supply store, there is a product called "shower board" or "tile board." This product is available in 8-foot sheets. Ask your local retailer if they will cut the product into handheld sizes for classroom use. If you mention that you're a teacher, the cutting fee may be waived. Your school can supply a tax-free letter to further reduce the cost.

Colorful Concoctions

Level 2 example

Usage: Small group instruction to teach main idea and/or comprehension skills and study skills, and to incorporate specific IEP requirements into the general education content.

Divide students into two groups. One group will work on a specific content skill with one teacher, and the other group will work with the other teacher on a reading comprehension strategy embedded in the content. After a timed interval, the groups will flip flop.

What you'll need for each student in the reading strategy group:

One page reading handout
Yellow highlighter
Blue highlighter

Day 1
Ask the students to put their name at the top of the page, and then highlight the main idea in each paragraph with the yellow highlighter.

Collect the yellow highlighters and distribute the blue ones.

Ask the students to highlight in blue exactly what you tell them to, which are the main ideas that should have been highlighted.

The passages where the yellow and blue highlighters overlap are now green.

Collect the papers and divide the papers into three groups: yellow, blue, and green.

The students whose papers are mostly yellow are lacking in brevity skills. They don't know how to pare down and look for small bits of information.

The students whose papers are mostly blue don't have a clue as to what "main idea" means. They need some "main idea" instruction.

The students whose papers are mostly green have mastered the "main idea" assignment. They would benefit from enrichment and extension activities.

Day 2
Now the students can be divided into three groups for tiered instruction:
The blue group can be given a quick 15-minute main idea exercise - with one teacher.
The yellow group can be given a 15-minute exercise on honing in - with one teacher.
The green group can do some targeted instruction practice for 15 minutes – working independently.

Six Stations with Interrupters instructions (cont'd from p. 57)

To implement this practice, create two teacher stations and four independent stations. Here is one example of how you might set up this co-teaching configuration:

- Station 1 is a teaching station where students receive direct instruction.
- Station 2 is independent reading, where students will read something, take some notes and respond to questions.
- Station 3 is an independent group – these students are writing a commercial based on an assigned topic. They have to come up with a 2-minute skit (or commercial) that highlights some of the key points that we've discussed.
- Station 4 is a teaching station for students to receive additional direct instruction from the second teacher.
- Station 5 is an independent station. The students have laptop computer work to do.
- Station 6 is a standing station. Students have concept cards and they have to sort them into different categories, as a pair.

Six stations with Interrupters example:

Imagine one rotating student named Susan.

- Susan receives instruction from the teacher at Station 1.
- After about fifteen minutes, she and the group rotate to the reading assignment at Station 2.
- Then we have a commercial break or interrupter. The students that were in Station 3 get up and do a two-minute commercial with some of the key ideas they were exposed to. They present to the entire class for two minutes. Susan watches.
- Susan rotates to Station 3 and she works on her commercial break.
- After fifteen minutes, she rotates to Station 4 for some teacher-led learning.
- We stop again, and there is another commercial break put on by some of the students. Susan's group performs their commercial for the class.
- Susan rotates to Station 5, then to Station 6, and then there is a third commercial break.

Research has shown that the interrupters give the brain an opportunity to absorb information. It doesn't have to be a commercial that students devise. Maybe you have a brief Internet video that illustrates key points of the lesson. It could be something humorous that breaks up the day. By providing opportunities to move around, you have included kinesthetic teaching.

Instead of a class of thirty students, you have six small groups of five, which allows for some skill drill, some assessment, or some targeted instruction.

You can combine any of these practices and create new hybrids that are personalized to the task at hand and the curriculum. Some teachers are more comfortable with one type of practice than another and may never try some of these techniques. The point is to have plenty of options to allow for maximum flexibility.

Pictures of co-teaching configurations

Mirror
(2 groups)

Each teacher teaches the **same objective at the same time (groups do not switch)**

Teacher 1 Group A	Teacher 2 Group B

Variations
- **Vary** groups through the use of **Differentiation**
- Apply different **Teaching Styles**
- Each group offers different **Learning Styles** or **Multiple Intelligences** options
- Vary by using differentiated **Assessments**

Flip/Flop
(2 groups)

After a timed interval, groups switch from one teacher to the other.

Two Objectives. Each teacher teaches a **Different Objective to their group**

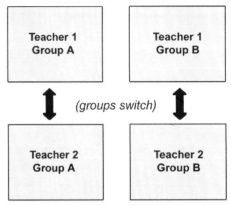

Variation
- Specific skill stations without flip/flop (2 different objectives based on data)

Flip/Flop Switch
(2 groups)

Two or three teaching objectives

Data based groups. Teacher 1 teaches the main lesson, Teacher 2 PRE-teaches the lesson. After an interval, groups switch.

The pre-taught group then receives the same lesson from Teacher 1.

The lesson group receives RE-teaching or ENRICHMENT from Teacher 2.

Teacher 1 (Main Lesson)   Teacher 2 (Pre-teach/ Re-teach/Enrich)

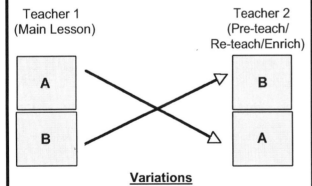

Variations
- Each group receives initial pre-teaching lesson based on data-driven decisions.
- Students receive initial lesson (mirror style) then students are regrouped for re-teaching purposes.

3 Station Rotation
(3 groups: two teacher groups and one independent group)

Three teaching objectives

Each teacher instructs a group, and a third group completes an independent activity. After a timed interval, the groups switch. The students participate in all three groups.

Note: In the independent group, students may work or sit: alone, in pairs, or as a group.

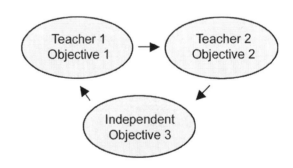

Variations
Three stations, but students only participate in two groups, with the following determined by the data:

- One teacher group and one independent group
- Two teacher groups, no independent group

3 Station Tiers
(3 groups: all teacher taught for some time)

One objective, tiered for maximum student success (NO Rotation)

Teacher 1 teaches the basic group (example: 20 minutes), Teacher 2 splits the same amount of time between the two other groups (example: 10 minutes teaching the intermediate group / then 10 minutes teaching the advanced group - teaching is alternated with independent work)

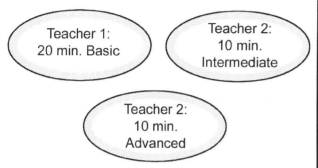

Variation

- Teacher 1 spends 20 minutes enriching the advanced group and Teacher 2 spends 10 minutes teaching the other two groups.

4 Station Rotation
(4 groups: 2 teacher taught, 2 independent)

Four objectives
Students spend time with each teacher and complete/participate in two independent tasks.

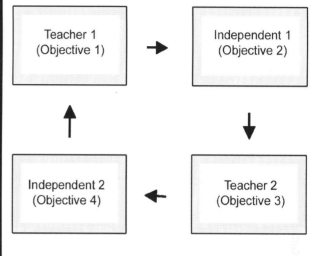

Variation

- Students may complete the rotations over two days instead of one.

4 Stations with one Teacher Flip/flop
(4 groups)

Two Objectives

The class is spit in half and each teacher alternates between an instructional group and an independent group. Students only see one teacher.

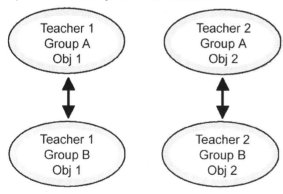

Variations

- Teachers have the same objective for each group
- Teachers have different objectives for each group based on student needs.

4 Stations with Tiers
(4 groups)

One objective (NO rotation by students)

Each group works with a teacher for a specified amount of time, then the teacher moves to a second group. The lesson content is the same, but the lesson is differentiated for the various ability group levels.

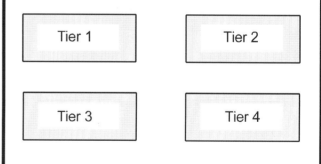

Variation

- You may have one basic, two intermediate and one advanced group or any other ability combinations that make sense.

6 Stations with Interrupters
(6 groups)

Six Objectives

Students rotate between six groups. Two are teacher taught and four are independent. This configuration may take more than one class period if you do not work in a block schedule.

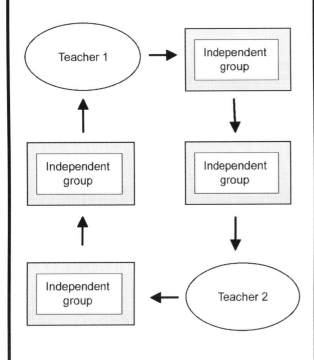

Variations

- Students may double up in one group, or skip a group if it is appropriate.

Skills Groups
(1 large group task and
2 small flexible mini groups)

Objectives vary by group (many objectives: individualized)

Students are given a whole group task. Each teacher siphons off one to six students at a time to offer a short (in duration) mini lesson. Students are then returned to the group at large and another mini lesson group is created.

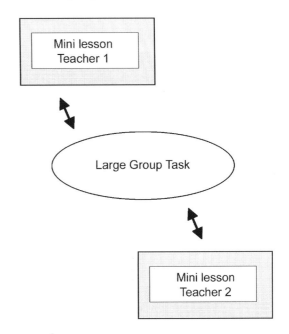

Variations

- The purpose of the group may include re-teaching, pre-teaching, conferencing, assessment, skill focus, collaboration, drill, behavioral practice or any other need, as determined by the teachers. Each group has its own purpose, make-up and duration.

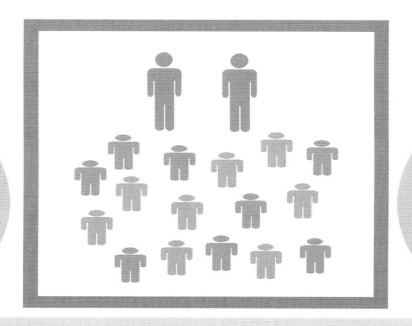

Advancing Your Use of Classroom Management for Co-Teaching

DOMAIN
4

Domain IV

Classroom Management

Classroom management comprises a variety of routines and procedures aimed at establishing a positive learning environment. To advance co-teaching practices, we must collaborate and co-examine our management techniques to create a unified approach in our classroom.

Co-teachers should discuss and agree on classroom rules. How will teachers enforce rules? What are your non-negotiables? Consider this: if one teacher feels chewing gum is intolerable and the other teacher allows students to chew gum – how will that affect your co-teaching relationship? Other areas to discuss are routines – items such as how students hand in papers, routines for lining up, or general routines, such as how and when to contact parents.

Co-teachers should also consider how to establish a positive classroom community. Discuss and agree upon procedures for dealing with and handling difficult behaviors. What are your "zero tolerance" parameters? Other factors to discuss might include bullying and behavior intervention plans.

Take a moment to reflect on each of your practices and negotiate one common routine for your co-taught classroom.

<table>
<tr><td colspan="3" align="center">**Assessment directions: Identify your co-teaching stages
and create ideas and plans to advance your practices**</td></tr>
</table>

	Classroom Management	
	Rules and routines, consistent expectations, community and relationship building	
Stage 1 Level 1	• Special educator assumes role of "behavior manager" so the general educator can 'teach' • Rules and routines have not been co-founded, one teacher's system is being utilized • Management strategies were not discussed or agreed upon, are done "on the fly" as needed	Ideas for Advancing Practices in Classroom Management:
Stage 2 Transition	• Increased communication and mutual development of rules and routines • Favor tends to rest with group approaches to management and not with individual behavior plans • Grouping configurations are used occasionally, some kinesthetic activities are offered each unit	
Stage 3 Level 2	• Both teachers are involved in developing and implementing a classroom management system • Individual behavior plans, use of contracts, tangible rewards, and reinforcers; community-building and relationship-building activities are common • *Positive Behavioral Supports* are evident on an ongoing basis • Proactive and communication strategies allow/create a positive learning environment for all students • Teaching in flexible groups with the use of kinesthetic activities is the instructional norm on a daily basis • Small, flexible groups include instruction in pragmatic, social and cooperative learning skills	

Data Collection

Level 1: Data collection (behavioral or academic or both)

Level 2: Use the data during planning sessions to create learning options

---

Some Response to Intervention Behavior Resources:

www.interventioncentral.com

www.easycbm.com

www.chartdog.com

www.rti.org

www.wrightslaw.com/info/rti.index.htm

www.rti4success.org

On pages 70-71 and 75-76, you will find various data collection charts to use in your classroom. Some charts are for collecting data for individuals, some are about collecting data for groups, some charts document behavioral data, and some charts document academic data.

Roster Recipe

Usage: Data Collection

You will want to be as efficient as possible with your data collection, so that you don't lose valuable instructional time to the task. Here's a strategy that will allow you to collect information quickly:

Make multiple copies of your classroom roster and put the copies in a folder or on a clipboard labeled Data Collection.

If there's a particular skill that you want to look at fairly consistently, write that skill at the top of one of the roster pages, along with the date. So if the skill is "Time On Task," you would label your roster page as such. That way, the kids' names are already there, ready to go, and you can begin collecting data on how they manage their time. Any time one teacher is supporting or facilitating using Level 1 practices, materials are ready for that teacher to take data while drifting around the class.

This gives you specific data to refer to, which can be especially useful in parent-teacher conferences. Sometimes parents do not understand the extent of an issue their child may demonstrate, but if you can point to exact data that show "on this date, this is how many minutes he spent on task," then they will know that you're not just singling out their child and maybe, together, parents and teachers can begin to address the issue at hand.

Another trick is to copy the roster list onto address labels. That way, you can write the data directly onto the label. When you need to consolidate data for one child, you can remove the label and place it in the student's file.

Data Collection

Example: Tally Charts. Count the number of incidences of a behavior or number of times a student demonstrates a skill.

Frequency Behavior Tally of an Individual's Behavior

Behavior of Student A	Day One (20 minutes)	Day 2 (20 minutes)
Blurts out of turn	卌 IIII	卌 卌 IIII

Frequency Task Tally for a Class Academic Skill

Student	Task: Identifies main idea and two details in a grade level paragraph (Main Idea = M, Detail = D)
Anderson	M, D, D
Cromwell	Needed directions twice, could only find details. D
Ing	M, D, D
Etc….	

Strategies for tally charts:

- Identify and describe the components of the task or behavior.

- Agree on a start and end time of the tally collection.

- Discuss the information at your next planning session.

- Collect the same information after an intervention has been embedded into the instruction.

- Have both teachers take turns with the tally charts.

Tally Chart

Student's name:

Identified goal of the data collection (how will the data be used):

Dates and time periods:

Data collector:

Behavior/Academic Skill	Data collection day one	Data collection day two

Analysis of data:

1. As a result of this data, our goal is to:

_____

_____

2. The intervention we will try is:

_____.

3. Follow-up will occur on: _____.

Second Helping

Usage: Behavior management

Here is one of my favorite strategies for managing a student whose behavior is a problem.

Imagine we're in the 3 Station Rotation. My co-teacher, Lenora, is teaching at one station, I'm teaching at another, and there's an independent station.

When Tommy Turnaround gets to that independent station, he does everything but work independently. He becomes a distraction to the kids in his station, and to the teacher-led stations as well.

Here's how you deal with this kind of situation: Tommy Turnaround starts with me and then he goes to Lenora. After that, instead of moving on to the independent station, he comes back to me and becomes my teaching assistant.

This can also be used to give a double dose of information to kids that need it. Depending on what the student needed more – a double dose of Lenora's lesson, or a double dose of my lesson – that's what he would receive.

So the second helping can be used as a re-teaching strategy, and also as a behavior management strategy. It is also a terrific technique for providing in-class interventions during core instruction in an RTI model.

A Few Thoughts on Higher Order Thinking Questions and Opportunities To Respond

Higher order thinking questions

It is very important for children with disabilities to practice higher order thinking (HOT) questions. Quite often teachers like to ensure success for SWD by asking them easy-to-answer or lower-level, more concrete questions. We have to help SWD practice those HOT questions in the classroom if we expect them to have increased outcomes in the high stakes tests. Sometimes in the name of success we think, "Well, I'll just ask him easier questions so he'll be able to answer them and won't be embarrassed." Co-teaching allows us to pre-teach some of the more sophisticated information so that SWD are capable of answering the higher order questions.

TAPS: Opportunities to respond

There are four ways in which students can respond in classrooms. To remember these techniques,
I use the mnemonic TAPS, which stands for: Total, Alone, Pairs, and Small groups.

Total
Everyone responds at the same time. Example: if all the students have a white board and you ask a question, they can all write the answer down on the white board and hold it up. That way, you can assess how many of the students know the answer.

Alone
You ask a question and one student is called on to answer the question. That's your lone response. You don't have information on whether the others knew the answer or not.

Pairs
This technique allows more response by providing each student with a learning partner to respond.

Small Groups
In Level 2 co-teaching, we use small group interaction and intimate group settings to allow for more discussion and student response.

The goal in co-teaching is to decrease our A's and increase our T's, P's, and S's in whatever combination makes sense.

Recipe For Success

Usage: Teaching specific behavioral expectations

If you are not getting the behavior you want from your students, it may be because they are not clear on what is expected of them. Sometimes we just have to explicitly explain behaviors to students.

Create a T-chart that describes the behavior for a particular activity. For this example, imagine that "silent reading" is something you do in your classroom. In one column, write what silent reading behavior looks like and in the other column, write what silent reading behavior sounds like.

Silent Reading	
What it looks like	*What it sounds like*
Eyes on the book	No talking
Turning a page every minute	The soft swish of paper

The more your students work in small teacher-led groups, the fewer behavior problems you will have. In some of my action research, I have seen a tremendous decrease in referrals to the Principal's office whenever small groups were used. There is less opportunity for students to go off-task, wander mentally, or get creative behaviorally when they're engaged by small group instruction.

Identify three strategies from this section that you might like to try. How can you advance your co-teaching practice in this area? On page 67, there's a chart with a note-taking column for your use – it's labeled "Ideas for advancing your practice." Use this chart to outline strategies and techniques you can implement to advance your co-teaching practice.

Interval data. Pick a time interval and record the behavior for that interval of time. You only record the behavior at that moment in time, not an average of the time. Example: If you choose a 5-minute interval, you record the behavior precisely at the 5-minute mark.

Data collection
Interval Examples

Behavior: Time on task

5-minute intervals, time on task of an __individual__

Symbols used: X = on task, O = off task

Target: Student G

Data collected by Mrs. Smith

10:00	10:05	10:10	10:15	10:20	10:25	10:30	10:35
X	X	X	X	X	O	O	O

Data analysis:

Goal: Improve time on task during the latter half of the period.

Strategies: Provide Student G with kinesthetic practice activities to maintain interest and attention. Increase the use of peer work.

Behavior: Time on task

5-minute intervals, time on task of a __class__

Number indicates number of students on task at the end of the interval out of 24 students

Class task: note taking, lecture and discussion

Data collected by Mr. Jones

10:00	10:05	10:10	10:15	10:20	10:25	10:30	10:35
23	23	20	16	12	10	14	17

Data analysis

Goal: Improve time on task

Strategy: Co-teach using 3 stations to allow for differentiated tasks in order to sustain attention.

Interval Data

Behavior to observe: _____

Interval time: _____

Symbols used and definitions: _____

_____

Target (student, class): _____

Data collector: _____

Time intervals:							

Data analysis:

_____

_____

Goal(s):

_____

_____

Strategy (strategies):

_____

_____

Dolci

Usage: More Ideas for Data Collection (Progress Monitoring)

Student behaviors and skills:

- Count the number of questions answered correctly

- Create a rating scale (quality of group participation, 1-5)

- Count demonstration/competency in a given skill (+ = yes, - = no)

- Monitor if a student works with little to no additional help (independent with skill, rate independence versus needing help)

Teacher behaviors and skills (for very advanced pairs, when comfortable)

- Count the types of questions asked by co-teacher (higher order thinking questions, question types)

- Count students that get called on in class (boy/girl ratio, all students called on, same students all the time…)

- Count the number of opportunities a student, or the class, has to respond. (Increased opportunities to respond = higher scores)

- Count the number or ratio of positive / reinforcing statements

Behavior Resources:

www.behaviordoctor.org

www.pbis.org

http://safeandcivilschools.com

Improve your "Opportunities To Respond" stats

On the previous page, there are some ideas for co-teachers to collect data on each other. This is only if you're an advanced pair, and only if you're both excited about the idea. In that case, you might collect data on each other's pedagogy.

This exercise is for advanced co-teaching pairs. Don't do this unless you're very comfortable with each other. But for those of you who are advanced, this might be a way for you to improve your practice through reflection and conversation.

Take turns scripting every question that your co-teacher asks and then go back and co-rate the questions according to Bloom's taxonomy (chart p. 121). Discuss the following questions:

- What kinds of questions do you ask?

- How many higher order questions do you ask?

Notice how your co-teacher decides which student to call on.

- Do you call on more boys than girls?

- Do you always call on the same kids?

- Do you call on kids that are on your left side versus your right side?

Think about how the students are engaged.

- How many opportunities to respond do we offer students?

- Are we getting seven to ten responses every ten minutes?

- After reflecting on this data, what ideas do we have for improving our practice?

Tempting Tasks

Usage: Teaching students to pay attention in class

Kids spend a lot of their time in school listening and paying attention, but how to pay attention and how to listen are skills we rarely teach. These are skills that the kids are simply expected to know.

At times, I teach a strategy called SLANT*, that I learned as a Strategic Instruction Model Professional Developer (University of Kansas).

SL – Sit up and lean slightly forward
Activate your thinking (think about what is being said)
Nod occasionally (and smile)
Track the Talker (visually turn to look at speaker)

In the co-teaching classroom, I explicitly teach behavior skills as a part of the small group instruction. Students practice, role-play and generalize specific behavior skills as a part of their classroom grade. This is another example of how co-teaching interfaces with RTI and – as in this example – with the behavior part of the RTI framework during core instruction.

Social skills help kids feel empowered and engage them in the classroom. When students demonstrate good listening skills, teachers feel students are benefiting from the lesson.

Credit: University of Kansas, Strategic Instruction Model
www.ku-crl.org

Case Study: SLANT

In high school, I had a student named Tim who had a talent for irritating my co-teacher.

Every day at the end of class, my co-teacher would visit me in my classroom to vent about Tim. Depending on the way her high heels sounded as she came down the hall--whether they were clipping or clopping--I could tell what kind of mood she was in. Invariably I could hear the storm brewing as she clopped down the hall, and then she would blow into the room and her frustration would come pouring down. Tim's behavior and non-compliance in the classroom really upset her.

Since Tim wasn't even attempting the warm-up assignments in class, we agreed that I should pre-teach him, along with a couple of other students. Instead of pre-teaching the lesson, I decided to teach the students SLANT* skills to help increase their attention and time on task. I taught them the technique through a series of mini-lessons during the first ten minutes of class. I approached Tim one day and said, "Here's the deal. All you have to do in class today is SLANT. You don't have to do another thing and that's all that I expect of you today."

After class, I heard my co-teacher coming down the hall, but this time her heels were clipping along because she was so happy.

"He was participating!" she exclaimed. "He was nodding and smiling. He didn't say a word but I could tell he was with me the whole time. I'm going to give him bonus participation points!"

Later when I saw Tim, I told him, "You received bonus participation points in class today."

Tim said, "Really? You never told me that if I did all that stuff you were trying to teach me that I could pass without doing any work."

I said, "Absolutely! That's what I'm here for." ;)

Fast forward a few years. Tim turned sixteen and quit school. I stopped hearing from him for about five years, but I found out later that he earned his GED, took the ASVAB and was eventually accepted into the U.S. Marine Corps.

One day at school, I was paged over the intercom: "Mrs. Kunkel, please report to the office." When I arrived, there was a present for me on the counter. If you've ever been a teacher and you get a present and it's not your birthday, you're definitely NOT excited, but worried – "What could be inside that box?" The secretary, on the other hand, was very excited and she said, "Look! You've got a gift!" I finally got up the courage to open it and inside was a cute little pewter candleholder with a tea light in it. There was a card from Tim with his phone number. So I called him up, and he told me all about his life since high school, which now included a wife and baby. I thanked him for the gift and asked him what made him think of me after all these years.

He said, "Mrs. Kunkel, do you remember teaching me that SLANT thing?

I said, "Yes, I do."

Tim said, "Mrs. Kunkel, I think of you every day because every day, we use that technique in the U.S. Marine Corps."

Case Study: SLANT Redux

By the time my student teacher arrived in November, I had already taught my students how to SLANT. All I had to say was "Slant," and it elicited this reaction from kids: Sit up, lean slightly forward, nod and smile, track the talker, and (if they were really doing it right) activate your mind.

My student teacher never questioned what was going on. All that he knew was that if I stood in front of the class and said "Slant," I got this reaction from the students.

One day, we were going on a field trip. I put him in charge of one bus and I was in charge of the other. We had to make an announcement about lunch. He borrowed the microphone from the bus driver and he said, "Okay, everybody, I need you to slant." And like magic, all the kids on the bus sat up, leaned forward, and gave him their attention.

The driver was amazed. He said, "What's slant and how do you get it?"
My student teacher said, "I don't know, but it works every time."

Of course, the way you get the appropriate response is through instruction. You just can't go back to your classroom tomorrow and say, "Okay, everybody slant," and expect the same reaction.

So far, we've covered The Basics of Co-Teaching, and we've looked at the first half of the rubric. We've looked at communication, physical arrangement, instructional presentation, and classroom management. Now we're going to explore Instructional Strategies for Differentiating Instruction, specially designed instruction, and how to target specific academic needs that a child may have.

Co-teaching is much like the dynamic of other famous historical pairs. Humorist Ernest Heineman (my father) shares this story…

Sherlock Holmes and Dr. Watson went on a camping trip. After consuming a good bottle of wine, they fell into a deep sleep. All of a sudden in the middle of the night, Sherlock woke up, startled. He shook his faithful friend and cried,

"Watson, I need you to wake up! Wake up!"

Watson awakened with a start and said, "What's wrong?"

Sherlock Holmes cried, "Dr. Watson, what do you see?"

The good doctor raised himself up on one arm, looked around and said, "I see stars."

Sherlock said, "What does that tell you?"

Dr. Watson scratched his head, cleared his throat, and intoned, "Well, horologically, I deduce that it is a quarter past three in the morning. Theologically, I can see that God is all-powerful, and we are small and insignificant. Meteorologically, I deduce we will have a lovely day tomorrow. What does seeing the stars tell you, Mr. Holmes?"

"Dr. Watson, it tells me that someone has stolen our tent."

Co-teaching brings two very different perspectives together to create a dynamic approach. In the following pages, we're going to continue with more strategies and more ways to be a dynamic duo.

Case Study: Chemistry Lesson

During a break in one of my seminars, a young teacher approached me with his co-teaching problem.

Teacher: "We have all these kids in chemistry, kids who have probably never taken chemistry before in their lives. So we have what we call integrated chemistry, which is ME and two regular chemistry teachers. I go between two classes during the same period, so we have four classes total: two periods, two classes each. I go back and forth, so obviously it's not ideal."

Sonya: "Can you think of another way to do it?"

Teacher: "This is just a kind of trial thing, and I think they're trying to find some way to provide immediate support."

Sonya: "Support, not instruction?"

Teacher: "I can't think of another way to do this. I feel pulled in too many directions."

Sonya: "I've co-taught in chemistry – you can, too. Pick an area of instructional focus - like vocabulary."

Teacher: "It's the back and forth between classes that's tough. If I stay in one class for a whole day, then what's happening to those other kids in the other class?"

Sonya: "Can you work it out with the teachers that they can stagger their lessons, so you can teach with teacher A one day, and teach the same lesson with teacher B the next day?

Teacher: "Ideally, we can talk to the administration and get away from having me in two rooms."

Sonya: "Or one teacher can be the chemistry co-teacher. What you're doing now is support. And I get that and I understand why and I understand the situation you're in, but if you want to advance your practices and you want to focus on instruction, then we have to put you in a situation where it can be instructional and not just about showing up. If nothing else, maybe you focus your instruction for one period a week. You know, Monday you do something with one teacher and Wednesday it's the other teacher. Maybe for the next year, you could reconfigure your schedule a little differently so that it isn't so disruptive. Monday, Tuesday, co-teach with one teacher. Wednesday, Thursday, teach with the other one. Then offer support to both classes for half periods on Fridays. I'm not really sure how you can advance your practices if you're running between two rooms, with the goal being to support instruction that students don't understand. Consider how you might design the instruction so that students learn at point of instruction."

Additional note: Co-teaching is best used for instructional purposes. It is better to co-teach well in one classroom than to be reactive to instruction that is not working in two classrooms.

Co-Teaching, Anyone?

Should co-teaching be voluntary? Maybe.

It is always best when adults have choice and voice in their assignments. Certainly, if someone volunteers, they are more likely to be invested in the process. But what do you do if no one volunteers, yet children need co-teaching services?

Co-teaching should not be the only service available for students with disabilities. However, as a service offered by a school district to parents at an IEP meeting, it should not depend on whether someone volunteers or not.

Advancing Your Curriculum Familiarity and Your Use of Differentiation of Instruction for Co-Teaching

DOMAIN 5

Domain V

Curriculum Familiarity and Differentiation of Instruction

In a class filled with students representing a large range of abilities, the struggle to meet core standards while maintaining rigor and creating access for all students is the major challenge most classroom teachers face. To advance practices, teachers need to collaborate regarding key standards, areas of instructional expertise, and areas of instructional weakness. How familiar are both teachers with key aspects of the curriculum? What differentiated practices will be used to differentiate process, product, or content?

By combining expertise (a content expert with a strategic instruction expert), how can co-teachers capitalize on each other's strengths to multiply the impact of instruction? It is <u>not</u> important that both teachers know the content or strategies equally. It <u>is</u> important that teachers reflect on the data and discuss how best to approach teaching with two certified individuals in the classroom to create a value-added opportunity for students.

**Assessment directions: Identify your co-teaching stages
and create ideas and plans to advance your practices.**

	Curriculum Familiarity & Differentiation (General Education) *Competency and confidence with the general education curriculum by both teachers*	
Stage 1 Level 1	• Special educator is unfamiliar with the content or methodology used by general educator • Lack of curricular knowledge creates lack of confidence in both teachers • General educator feels reluctant to "hand over the chalk" to special educator • Special educator feels it's difficult to make suggestions for accommodations & modifications • Special educator and general educator do not exchange materials regularly or in a timely fashion	Ideas for Advancing Practices with Curriculum Familiarity:
Stage 2 Transition	• Confidence with curriculum grows • General educator is more willing to modify the curriculum or accept modifications from special educator • Both teachers share accommodation and modification responsibilities	
Stage 3 Level 2	• Both teachers appreciate the specific curriculum competencies that each bring to the content area • All aspects of teaching are now jointly and comfortably shared • Demonstrated balance between curriculum and IEP objectives and needed strategies • Conversation and decisions have been made by the teachers regarding roles when curriculum familiarity is in question • Modifications are available to ANY student that needs them	

Curriculum Supports: Level 1 Co-Teaching

An important part of curriculum support is the infusion of kinesthetic activities.

Level 1 kinesthetic activities make learning fun and they also multiply the impact of instruction. The key is to ensure that all students can experience success with the activity. One way to achieve that is to give the group a couple of minutes at the beginning of a task to do some quick strategizing about how they're going to accomplish the activity. Co-teachers can guide students in determining whether some of them might be struggling with the task. They can then offer some suggestions or ideas, which reduces the anxiety that struggling students often feel when engaging in an activity. When the activity begins, the students participate in the activity in a meaningful way that is fun and effective for everyone.

Competitions of all kinds are a popular kinesthetic activity. This might consist of students coming up to the board or passing things around very quickly in a circle. There are even story relays: one student writes the beginning of a story on a piece of paper and the next student adds two more sentences, and so on. The group has five minutes to develop a group story that makes sense, which teaches students how one sentence flows into the next and also how to use good transition words.

On the next page, you'll see an example of another good Level 1 strategy - a VIP or Visual Instruction Plan, which helps students get set up in an activity. The VIP outlines how students can approach a task and gives them kind of a holistic view and a list of what they're going to be expected to do.

Visual Instruction Plans

The VIP has three specific components:

1. Lists five or six steps (no more than six) that are clearly described.

2. Uses very few words.

3. Has pictures. When students with disabilities or students who are English language learners (ELL) go back to remember the steps, they might not remember the words. They're more likely to remember the visuals of VIP presentations.

VIPs show students the steps needed to accomplish the task and its important components. Try to pinpoint where the task becomes difficult for the child with disabilities, and write the VIP accordingly. Hand the students the VIP before a lesson, task or activity. Preview the steps with students in a small group. A VIP can be a powerful tool before, during and after instruction. See the example VIP on the next page.

Use VIPs during instruction to help students understand and remember instructional sequences.

Level One supports: Visual Instruction Plans – Level One Example
(Accommodation Support)
ASC answer-support-connect

A method to help you answer **open-ended questions** when you have to **form an opinion** and **support with details**

STEP 1: Make sure you understand the question.

What does the question ask?

STEP 2: Look at the **key words** in the question

WORDS

STEP 3: **Think** about it and form an opinion

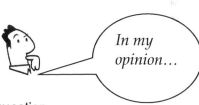

In my opinion…

STEP 4: Answer the question using some of the key **words** in the question

STEP 5: Support your answer with **details** from the **text** and your **personal experiences**

BE SURE TO INCLUDE SOME OF
THE WORDS FROM THE TEXT

- Detail
- Detail
- Detail

Question → *Answer*

STEP 6: **Connect** your details to the original question

REMEMBER to SHOW how the question and answer **relate**.

Your completed answer should be 3 or 4 sentences.

Mix & Match Activity

Level 1 Activity (Two Facilitate)

Creating a Prediction (improving comprehension skills) and Differentiation for Various Reading Levels

Example: Level 1

Simmer and Stir

Usage: Level 1 co-teaching example of Differentiation of Instruction to account for a variety of reading levels AND the infusion of Specially Designed Instruction in reading comprehension.

When introducing a new text, teachers often read aloud to the class and then stop and ask a question. Unfortunately, in that case the teacher is doing all the thinking by coming up with the question, and the students are robotically responding to a teacher initiation.

The following exercise engages students directly with the text and provides a kinesthetic activity while they practice forming a prediction or hypothesis. Students will be taking information and making an educated guess based on the information they have in front of them. It can be adapted to any reading level. It also serves as differentiated instruction for students with low reading ability.

What you'll need:
Seven to ten key quotes or excerpts from a section of text, typed up on color-coded 3 x 5 cards. (All of the yellow cards have the first quote, all of the blue cards have the second quote, etc.)

How to mix and match:

1. Divide the cards among the students.

2. Ask the students to guess what the reading selection will be about, based upon the quote on their index cards. Have them write down their predictions on a graphic organizer or in a journal.

3. Now the students pair up with someone who has a different color card. They read each other their predictions, they read each other's quotes, and with this new information, they discuss what they think the reading selection will be about, and they write down their new predictions.

4. After two minutes, they mix it up again and find someone with a card of another color. They pair up with this new person, read each other's quotes and predictions, and discuss what the book might be about.

5. Have the students complete two more rotations and then return to their seats.

6. The teacher reads aloud the quotes and/or excerpts that were taken from the section of text (the students are just listening and do not have a copy of the text). Interest will be high because students will be curious to find out how their quotes fit into the text.

7. Have the students view the text. Get them in pairs and have them pick up reading where the teacher left off. Ask them to stop at the end of every page or paragraph and continue to make predictions throughout the rest of the chapter.

It's not really important that students read all the words in a text, but it is important that they learn how to utilize the text. This is a very effective way of teaching reading comprehension strategy. Students stop at various points and make a prediction, then they go back and review their predictions once they finish the chapter. Reading comprehension can be increased, even if the student can't read all the words.

That is what's important about giving students access to materials.

This exercise differentiates instruction, helping students to focus on the facts in these authentic materials. The kinesthetic nature of the activity doesn't require a huge effort to set up, and does not distract them from learning. It does provide the kinesthetic learner an opportunity to learn and respond through the strength of their learning style.

Special Ingredients

Usage: Support students with memory difficulties by providing independence.

In my classroom, I keep a shoebox that holds the outlines for various activities written on large index cards. On one side of the card is the name of the activity, for instance, "Adding Decimals." On the flip side, there is a description of how you add decimals with a step-by-step example.

If I'm teaching mathematics and I have students that can't remember how to add decimals, they can get up and go through the box and take the recipe cards back to their desks. Students with disabilities need help processing the small details. The recipe cards help them remember the skill that they either never mastered or can't recall. The cards serve as a memory device.

Another kind of VIP is a video made with a flip cam or other recording device. I once worked with a science teacher who was co-teaching with a technology teacher and they were working on an integrated unit on building bridges. The technology teacher taped himself performing an assembly task and it was on a VCR that was available for the students. The tape described how to put something together step-by-step. The students could review it repeatedly – watch it, stop, see what he did, watch it, stop it, do what he did…

Another VIP option takes advantage of the fact that many of the students in your classroom have cell phones in their pockets (which, of course, they're not supposed to have). Many of them have iPhones and androids that have video capability. If you ask, "Does somebody have a cell phone so they can videotape me giving directions to the whole group?" you'll probably get lots of volunteers. When the kids get in their groups, they can play the directions back. Could you post the video on your teaching website? That way, students can refer to them while at home doing their homework?

If you need guidance on creating VIPs, a good resource is the Tools for Teaching website: www.FredJones.com, which has some really good examples.

Frequently asked question regarding Level 2 curriculum and expertise:

"If a co-teacher is not teaching the curriculum…..then what?"

Special education teachers can teach many aspects of curricula. Nevertheless, there are times where it's best to let the content expert teach the curriculum. Conversely, there are times when content teachers are at a loss as to how to embed or approach strategic instruction.

When not teaching a specific curriculum, a co-teacher can always teach strategies!

Teaching Strategies List

TEACH STRATEGIES!!!!

- Reading Strategies….
- Fluency Strategies…..
- Writing Strategies….
- Math Calculation Strategies….
- Math Processing Strategies…..
- Memory Strategies…..
- Executive Function Skills…..
- Study Skills…..
- Pragmatic Skills….
- Behavior Skills….
- Vocational Skills….
- Social Skills…..

Let's use the 3 Station Rotation as an example. One group can work with the general education teacher on curriculum, the specialist can work with students on a reading strategy, and the third group can work independently.

Independent groups can be constructed in many ways. Here are three different ways independent groups can be managed: as whole groups, as pairs, or as individuals. Choose the best process for your classroom.

Level 2: Strategies for Independent Groups

Groups – students sit as a group and work together on:

- Study routines
- Vocabulary sorting
- Brainstorming with technology (www.inspiration.com or www.kidspiration.com)
- Building, making or creating projects
- Playing learning games
- Activities at standing stations

Peer Work – Students are assigned a study partner and they sit as pairs

- Peer practice – students practice together
- Peer reciprocal reading – students take turns reading
- Flash card, foldable skills practice – students use a variety of tools, like flash cards, to practice skills.

Alone/independent work – students work alone and can sit anywhere in the classroom.

- Illustrations – creating drawings
- Vocabulary work – practicing vocabulary
- Book work
- Worksheets

When creating your independent groups, consider the management strategies you will need to employ in order for students to remain on task. Your number one strategy is to plan respectful tasks (page 97) and not busywork. See the next page for management tips.

Tips for Managing Independent Groups in Level 2

- At the station, have directions spelled out for the independent group.

- Have predetermined start and end times, written down.

- Prepare "sponge" activities for early finishers.

- Assign one student as the independent group manager. Prepare them at the beginning of class before the groups start with directions and task overviews.

- Post rotation signs on the board (time, direction).

- Create independent work that is self-correcting.

- Allow students to work in pairs on study activities.

- Post pictures of various desk configurations and refer to them. *Example: "We are going to be working in the 'Mini Lesson' groups today. Refer to the Mini Lesson diagram. Please move your desks as shown in the diagram."*

- Have a visual timer for the independent group.

- Post behavior rules or recipes for independent groups (see page 74).

- Have the independent group do meaningful review work, so as not to create anxiety or tension in students (which can lead to behavioral difficulties).

- Teach students to not interrupt the teacher while mini-lessons are "in action."

- Use the independent groups to provide <u>kinesthetic</u> opportunities.

> If you can't have kids sit together as a group because they do not behave well, you can have them work in pairs, or sprinkle them throughout the classroom. Choose what works for your classroom and your situation.

Calorie Saving
Combinations

Usage: Foster independent work behaviors in independent groups.

Sometimes kids at an independent station aren't terribly independent. If you let them, they will run to you, each in turn, with questions they probably could have answered themselves if they'd thought about it for a few moments.

One way to keep from being constantly interrupted while teaching your group is to designate one student as the group captain. Kids respond well to that kind of leadership responsibility. If any student has a question, he has to ask the captain. The captain becomes the representative for the student body and is the only student who can approach the teacher.

If you have four stations (two teacher-led and two independent groups) then one independent station is assigned to one teacher, and the other group refers to the second teacher. It minimizes chaos.

Another possibility is to use a "parking lot" between the independent groups. Kids who have specific questions can write them down on sticky notes and attach them to the item you have designated as the parking lot, such as a white board. During the rotation, one co-teacher can grab the questions and answer them for the whole class.

Ideas for Independent Stations

Around The Room (Carousel Brainstorming)
Place chart paper on the walls around the room. Each chart has a question that needs brainstorming. You divide the students by the number of charts into small groups. Each group is assigned a starting point, and then they go from chart to chart and they brainstorm each question in turn. Give students a clipboard with paper so that they can record their ideas. This is a great kinesthetic idea that gets them up and moving. It also encourages good dialogue and reflection.

COW's or Computers On Wheels
Use mobile laptop stations for your group work.

Illustrate It!
Students illustrate, draw or depict to practice various objectives.

Pairs Compare
Pairs of students work together to create and learn; then they compare their work with another pair.

Study Buddy
You give students a list of things they should know and then they pair off and quiz each other on the questions and record their buddy's answers. At the end of the exercise, they exchange sheets. That way, they can see what questions they missed and know what they need to study. A variation is to collect the quiz papers and use the results to form targeted study groups.

Organize this!
Students take time to organize desk, binder or study requirements per teacher's directions.

Kinesthetic ideas
Provide opportunities for students to create various products. Examples – using flash cards, sticky notes, create 'foldables,' etc.

Learning Styles Groupings
Some kids relate to words on the page, and those students will be taught in a documents-based group. Other kids find it hard to sit still, and will respond to a kinesthetic activity created from those same materials. For your visual learners, you might consider using maps, charts and graphs. Although the approach will be different for each independent group, the goal is for all the students to derive similar understandings of the topic.

For more information on co-teaching practices, strategies,
and for additional resources, please see my website:

www.KunkelConsultingServices.com

Notes Page

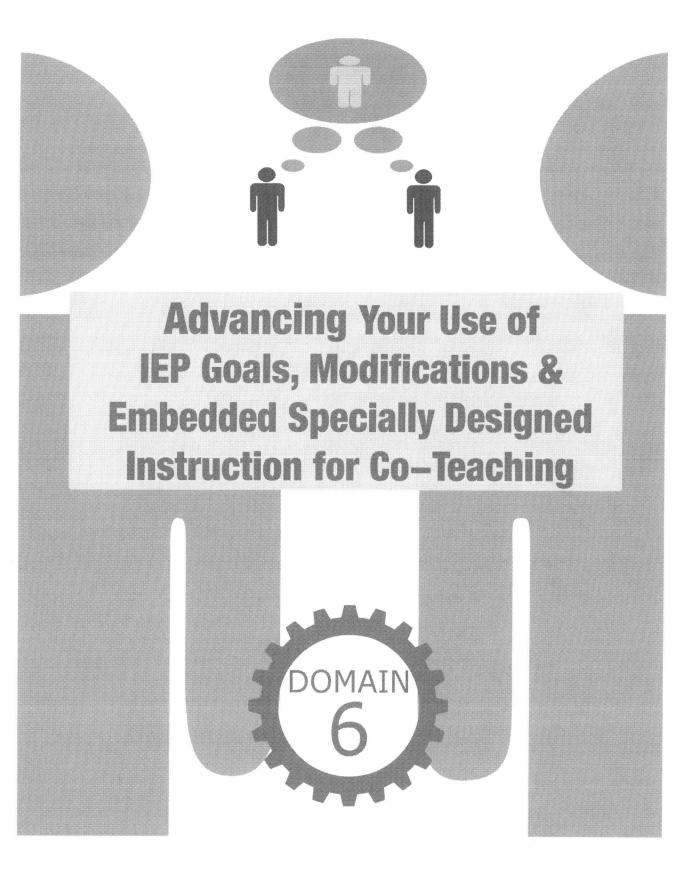

Advancing Your Use of IEP Goals, Modifications & Embedded Specially Designed Instruction for Co-Teaching

DOMAIN 6

Domain VI

Specially Designed Instruction

Co-teaching provided by a special education teacher may be considered part of a child's required service time as prescribed on an IEP. The co-teaching process should include how a student's goals and/or objectives are addressed through the curriculum. Co-teaching is MORE THAN a support. Many students benefit from support provided through accommodations and modifications – but that does not go far enough to meet a child's needs in a co-taught classroom. Students with disabilities would receive their accommodations and/or modifications even if co-teaching was not the service delivery model.

So – what else does co-teaching provide? It provides an opportunity to teach specific skills, as prescribed in the IEP, embedded in the curriculum to increase a child's independence. For example: a student needs to improve comprehension skills, per their goals. In the co-teaching classroom, the student receives specific instruction in comprehension strategies while learning the curriculum. Specially designed instruction is the process of focusing on the instructional design of the lesson that will create that opportunity for students.

Co-teaching serves the purpose of delivering a student's IEP goals through the general education classroom. How are you embedding these goals into your co-teaching practice?

	IEP Goals, Modifications and Specially Designed Instruction (special education)	**Ideas for Advancing Practices With IEP Goals, Modifications and Specially Designed Instruction:**
	Planning of the specific goals, objectives, accommodations and modifications for each student	
Stage 1 Level 1	• Programs are driven by textbooks and standards • IEP goals are addressed elsewhere (not in the general education classroom) • Modifications & accommodations are restricted to only those students with IEP's • Modifications are perceived as "watering down" the curriculum • Special educator is viewed as "helper" in the classroom • There is little interaction between co-teachers regarding modifications to curriculum • General educators may not realize that some students require modifications to content and they are responsible for these modifications too	
Stage 2 Transition	• General educator accepts accommodations, but prefers not to modify • The lesson in the co-taught classroom mirrors the same routine and instructional procedure as the other general education class • Differentiated instruction is used occasionally • Learning strategies are added in occasionally	
Stage 3 Level 2	• Both teachers are able to differentiate concepts that all students must know (big ideas) from concepts that most students should know (essential knowledge) • Accommodations for and modifications to content, activities, homework assignments, and tests become the comfortable norm for ALL students who require them - proactively planned • It is clear that both educators have planned accessible lessons and discussed exposure versus mastery of concepts for particular students. • IEP goals are embedded into lesson design • Learning styles regularly considered in lessons • Learning strategies are used regularly and emphasized	

Specially designed instruction aims to foster maximum independence by teaching a student specific skills. Rather than sorting students into homogeneous tiers, students can learn skills in heterogeneous groups. One way to group students is according to learning styles. When instruction is tailored to students' areas of strength, it helps them access the content and become more independent at managing and generalizing key information.

Pasta Tricolore

Usage: Visual, tactile and kinesthetic learning styles

Tactile learners process information through touch. If you incorporate three-dimensional learning aids, you will dramatically increase a student's ability to understand the lesson.

- Color coded sticky flags can be used in exercises that require underlining.

- Highlighting tape is fun for students to use as they complete an assignment that requires color-coding. For instance, color-code vocabulary words in yellow and key graphics in blue. At the end of the exercise, kids can return the highlighting tape pieces to a 3 x 5 laminated card, so that it can be reused.

Visual learners process information best through visual stimulation.

- Wet-erase markers can be used on worksheets inserted into sheet protectors for multiple practice opportunities.

- Variation: use a clear clipboard with wet-erase markers.
  Have student place a coversheet face down on a clear clipboard. By turning the clipboard over, students use their wet-erase markers to complete their task.
  When they are done, they can remove the worksheet and use it again for a second practice opportunity.

Specially Designed Instruction Ideas

Reading Comprehension

Here are some simple ideas to help students who struggle with accessing difficult reading materials, due to the discrepancy between their reading ability and the reading level of the text. These easy-to-implement techniques help students who struggle with reading participate in the curriculum.

The Sticky Note strategy

Visualize for a moment what it's like being in 2nd grade and having to read the kindergarten book because you have reading difficulties. You're embarrassed to pull out your book while everybody else is talking about a popular title. Here's what you can do so that your challenged readers can join in the conversation with their peers:

- For every page, create a sticky note that sums up the text in one simple sentence.
- Write the page numbers on the notes and stick the notes into a manilla folder.
- When a child wistfully sighs and wishes she could read what everyone else is reading, hand her the folder for that book.
- The child places the sticky notes on the pages where they belong in the book and she's able to read a text that would otherwise be beyond her reach. She may then be able to be part of a guided reading group on that particular book.

Using "Autosummarize"

In Microsoft Word (2007 or older), there's a nifty function that I find very helpful for teachers and students alike. In your command panel, find and enable "AutoSummarize." When you click on it, you are given four options. The first option automatically highlights the key points of your document for you. This can help students when they're doing research projects and they don't know how to glean the key concepts.

The other three buttons create an executive summary or abstract from your original document. These summaries can be very useful for pre-reading and main idea activities.

Readability Check

Microsoft Word will rate the readability of your document according to the Flesch-Kincaid readability index. To access this function, go to "Spelling and Grammar." Click on the button "Options" at the bottom of the dialogue box. That brings up another window. Under "Grammar," you need to check the boxes "Check grammar with spelling" and "Show readability statistics." To use this feature, select a sentence or paragraph, and then select Spelling and Grammar. The program will check the grammar and when you're done, you will be asked if you want to check the rest of the document. Click "no" and it brings up a window with your readability statistics. This paragraph, for instance, is rated a 7.8 grade readability level.

You can check the readability of everything, including tests, and you can simply adjust readability by shortening sentences and replacing the multi-syllabic words with simpler synonyms, which are accessed by right-clicking on a word.

The above paragraph was rated a 12th grade readability level because of the length of the sentence. You can quickly lower the readability level by chopping up sentences. The paragraph below is now rated at an 8.2 grade readability level. If I changed multi-syllabic to "words with two or more syllables," the readability level is lowered to 7.1.

You can check the readability of everything, including tests. You can simply adjust readability by shortening sentences. You can also replace multi-syllabic words. If you right click on the word, you'll get a list of synonyms.

Pesce del Giorno
"Fish of the Day"

Usage: Specially Designed Teaching Instruction to achieve
student independence in reading and writing tasks.

Instead of performing the readability check yourself, teach this technique to your students. That way, they can modify their own work if they need to.

When a student types up a writing paper and wants my help editing it, I say, "Run a readability check on that. Let's find out at what grade level you wrote this." After completing that task, the student says, "This is a 5.2," and I say, "Well, I'm a 9th grade teacher, I want to read 9th grade work." Then I suggest, "Why don't you do this: fix up your vocabulary and use some words other than 'said.' Then try combining sentences so that you turn simple sentences into compound or complex sentences," (and I demonstrate how to do that,) "and ramp up your readability. Then we'll talk about editing." The student comes back with the report and now it's a 9.2. So what is this student learning in the process? Editing skills. To paraphrase the old Chinese proverb: "Give a kid a fish, he eats for a day. Teach a kid to fish, he eats for a lifetime." That's what specially designed instruction is all about.

**Delectable
Dishes**

Usage: Academic activity for independent groups

Here is an independent group strategy that requires little to no prep, and kids love it.

What you'll need per group:
- 1 Zip-lock bag
- 5 or 6 little props (inside the plastic bag)

At home, raid a drawer that is cluttered with junk (pieces of Lego, broken toys, a pencil, a ruler, a cork). Portion out half a dozen of these meaningless treasures per bag.

Divide your independent group students into pairs. Have them come up with mini-commercials that explain all the important points they learned yesterday (or this week), using all the props in the bag.

Kids come up with crazy narratives that act as information attachment points. There was one kid that stuck a cork on the end of a ruler, and that was supposed to represent Admiral Dewey at the battle of Manila Bay. It sounds silly, but he was able to remember the details on the next test.

I call this strategy a Delectable Dish because the students are dishing out all the learning, and all I have to do is relinquish the clutter in my kitchen drawers.

Math Antipasti

Usage: Charts to help with math basics

Multiplication Chart:

	1	2	3	4	5	6	7	8	9	10	11	12
1	1	2	3	4	5	6	7	8	9	10	11	12
2	2	4	6	8	10	12	14	16	18	20	22	24
3	3	6	9	12	15	18	21	24	27	30	33	36
4	4	8	12	16	20	24	28	32	36	40	44	48
5	5	10	15	20	25	30	35	40	45	50	55	60
6	6	12	18	24	30	36	42	48	54	60	66	72
7	7	14	21	28	35	42	49	56	63	70	77	84
8	8	16	24	32	40	48	56	64	72	80	88	96
9	9	18	27	36	45	54	63	72	81	90	99	108
10	10	20	30	40	50	60	70	80	90	100	110	120
11	11	22	33	44	55	66	77	88	99	110	121	132
12	12	24	36	48	60	72	84	96	108	120	132	144

If you have students that can't memorize the multiplication facts, try a different tactic. Some kids can't learn the facts outside of context. This chart is great for students taking the high stakes test. On the parts where they can't use a calculator, if they can reproduce a 12 x 12 multiplication chart, they'll have a tool that can help them. To reproduce the tool, all they have to do is be able to count to 12 and do some simple addition. (see the next page)

How to fill out the multiplication chart

Kids learn very quickly how to do this.

First, have them fill in the top horizontal row and the left vertical row with the numbers in numerical order, leaving the top left square empty.

- To get the value of the first horizontal and vertical rows (the 1's), just copy the horizontal and vertical values (numbers 1-12)
- To get the values of the second horizontal row (the 2's), double the values of the first row (double the 1's row).
- To get the values of the third horizontal row (the 3's), add the values of the first two horizontal rows (add the 1's plus 2's).
- To get the values of the fourth row (the 4's), double the numbers in the second row (double the 2's).
- To get the values of the fifth row (the 5's), add the numbers in the second and third rows (add the 2's plus 3's).
- To get the values of the sixth row (the 6's), double the numbers in the third row (double the 3's).
- To get the values of the seventh row (the 7's), add the numbers in the third and fourth row (add the 3's plus 4's)

- Continue the pattern for the rest of the table. Note that for the odd numbered rows, you add the sum of the previous rows that make that number. For the 3's, you add the 1's + 2's. For the 5's, you add the 2's + 3's. For the 7's, you add the 3"s + 4's, etc.

Once students have this in front of them, they have a reference that can help them not only with multiplication and division, but also with fractions.

Fraction Equivalents: (Refer to the multiplication chart on page 106)
Let's say the fraction is 12/16. Find 12/16 vertically under the 4's column. Follow both rows back to the far left and you get the lowest equivalent fraction: ¾.
Fraction Equivalents – finding lowest values:
Now find the fraction 10/20 vertically under the 5. Follow the numbers far left horizontally and you get 2/4. We know that 2/4 can be reduced further still, because if you look under the 2 column and you see 2/4, you go to the left and get the lowest equivalent fraction: ½.

Integers Chart:

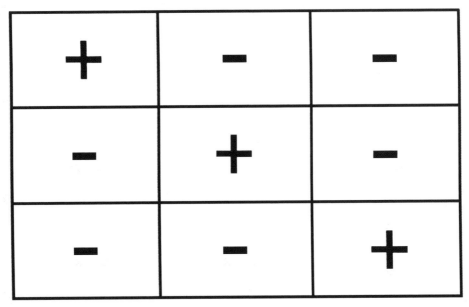

If you have students who have difficulty with multiplying and dividing positive and negative integers, this strategy will teach them the concept in under fifteen minutes, so that you can move on to more important curriculum objectives.

Have the students create a graphic organizer that looks like a tic-tac-toe. Have them place positive signs in all the boxes on one diagonal, and then fill in the rest of the boxes with negative signs. Presto! They now have all the rules for multiplying and dividing positive and negative integers.

- A positive multiplied/divided by a negative equals a negative (across the top row + - -)
- A negative multiplied/divided by a positive equals a negative (across the second row - + -)
- A negative multiplied/divided by a negative equals a positive (across the third row - - +)
- A positive multiplied/divided by a positive equals a positive (left to right diagonal +++)

This chart works in every direction!

Daily Specials

Usage: Teachers share modified materials stored in an online file cabinet

One way to minimize the workload that's associated with creating modifications and accommodations is to create an online repository. Many districts offer shared cyberspace that can host a virtual file cabinet for teachers' use. Create a folder system and deposit copies of modified materials by category. Be sure to share access codes (such as passwords) with all teachers and encourage them to add material as it is created.

To get started with your online file cabinet, create a primary folder called "Modifications."

Subfolders can be created for each area of study, such as "English" and "Mathematics."

Folders with modified material are organized by grade level. In this example, a 9th grade teacher has accessed the modifications for the first chapter of "To Kill A Mockingbird" by Harper Lee.

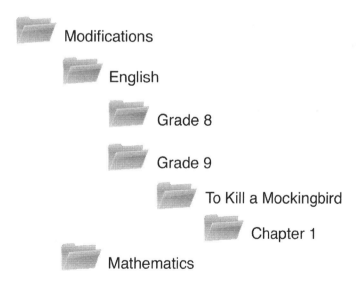

By storing all of your accommodations and modifications in this way, you can save time by not having to constantly reinvent new modifications. Over time, there is little work to be done to modify. This creates more time for focusing on instruction.

Regional Specialties

Usage: Flip Flop with Specially Designed Instruction –
A Mapping Strategy (Study Skills)

This is a labeling strategy that I used co-teaching in the Spanish 1 where the students were expected to be able to identify certain countries. A lot of the kids I work with have visual/motor integration issues and they don't understand a map. Colored pencils don't work because for them, this is a disorganized process. Through co-teaching, you can organize the process by providing students with a strategy that allows them to be independent without modifications.

What you'll need for each student:
• A map of South America
• A wet erase marker
• A clipboard and a clear plastic page protector that can be marked on
  …or a clear clipboard that can be marked on (map attached to back - see page 102)

When you're labeling diagrams, the first step is to start with an identifier. In this particular case, the country at the top of the continent is kind of shaped like a V, and it just so happens that's Venezuela. Now everybody takes their markers and they put a dot in Venezuela because that's their starting point.

Step 1. Put a dot on Venezuela.

Step 2. Using Venezuela as the starting point, draw a roadmap that passes through Colombia, Ecuador, Peru, Brazil, Paraguay, Uraguay, Argentina, Chile and Bolivia. The roadmap is in the shape of the letter S, for South America.

Step 3. Have students create a mnemonic to help them remember the countries that follow along the letter S. (This is what my students came up with: Very cold elephants put big pretty underwear around children's bottoms.)

So now they have a sequential structure with which to approach what appeared to them at first to be a random task.

That's specially designed instruction. What student doesn't benefit from a quick mapping strategy? In the co-teaching classroom, this can take place in one teacher-led station using Flip-Flop. For example: one group works with the general education teacher on important cultural aspects of South America and the other group works with the co-teacher on this strategy – after 15 minutes, students flip-flop groups.

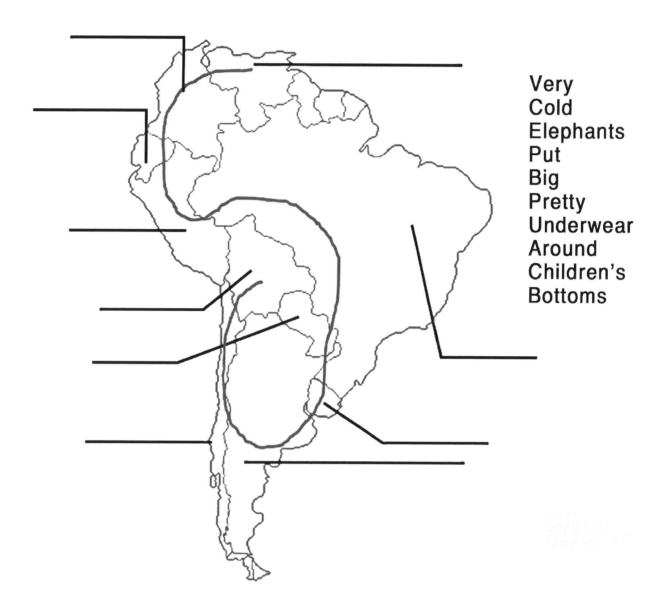

Very
Cold
Elephants
Put
Big
Pretty
Underwear
Around
Children's
Bottoms

Notes Page

Advancing Your Use of Instructional Planning for Co-Teaching

DOMAIN
7

Domain VII

Instructional Planning

"The idea of differentiating instruction to accommodate the different ways that students learn involves a hefty dose of common sense, as well as sturdy support in the theory and research of education (Tomlinson & Allan, 2000). It is an approach to teaching that advocates active planning for student differences in classrooms."
www.caroltomlinson.com

One of the most important components of successful co-teaching is co-planning. Co-planning means reaching consensus of how co-teachers will work together in the classroom to deliver core instructional objectives. Advanced co-teachers plan curriculum, materials usage, differentiation, data usage, teaching roles, management tasks, configurations, physical arrangement and assessment practices.

Co-planning is a commitment. Co-teachers must commit time to each other and the co-planning process. Co-teachers that forego planning are usually unable to advance their practices.

To ensure an effective-yet-brief co-planning session, exchange materials in advance of your meeting. It is a time-consuming process to show up to a co-planning session saying, "What are we going to teach tomorrow?" What you want to say is, "You gave me the materials and I read the lesson plan and I already pre-read the chapter so now let's talk about how we can differentiate this, or what Level 2 configuration can we use, or what's the best way to roll this out in Level 1?" The fundamental question should not be, "What are we going to teach," but "How will we approach our tasks?" If you arrive prepared for your co-planning meeting, you can plan a lesson in less than ten minutes.

The content specialist may discuss learning objectives, while the special education teacher suggests ways to meet the various needs of individuals within the classroom. Deciding ahead of time on each teacher's role helps the classroom run smoothly.

On pages 116 and 117, you'll find a Level 1 Planner. On page 120, there is a Level 2 Planner for any of the advanced configurations. You will also find a few examples of advanced lesson ideas on pages 125 and 126. For more sample lessons, please refer to my website:

www.KunkelConsultingServices.com

Work smarter, not harder...

Tip: It is easier for teachers to plan Level 2 lessons for their respective instructional groups than it is to plan a coordinated Level 1 lesson with both teachers in sync for the entire lesson.

Take a moment to reflect on your instructional planning practices.
What do you need to advance your practice?

Assessment directions: Identify your co-teaching stages and create ideas and plans to advance your practices

	Instructional Planning	
	Involves the on-the-spot, day-to-day, week-to-week, and unit-to-unit planning of coursework	
Stage 1 Level 1	• Planning is rare and "on the fly" • Separate curricula do not parallel each other • The general educator teaches the group, the special educator assumes the role of helper • The special educator works predominantly with students with disabilities • Only one teacher has a set of plans or materials • Level 1 co-teaching options are the norm	Ideas for Advancing Practices in Instructional Planning:
Stage 2 Transition	• There is more give and take in the planning process • Increase in time spent planning together • Plans are made explicating outline, both teachers' roles in the classroom (and paraprofessional roles as applicable) • Occasionally use Level 2 options over the course of the week	
Stage 3 Level 2	• Planning is now regular, ongoing and fully shared • Teachers continually planning, outside as well as during the instructional lesson • Teachers are able to comfortably change course during instruction to meet struggling learners' needs • Mutual planning/shared ideas are now the comfortable norm • Planning includes IEP goals and objectives being addressed through the curriculum • Level 2 co-teaching options are a regular part of the plan • Both teachers have a set of plans and materials, which reflect the curriculum, accommodations, modifications and IEP goals.	

Level 1 Co-Teaching Planner Page 1

Date	Standards/Objectives:
What will students be able to Know, Understand and Do? K U D	Differentiation:
IEP Goals to Consider:	How student will respond: (TAPS) Total Alone Pairs Small Cooperative Groups

Level 1 Configuration _____

- ☐ Speaker and Writer
- ☐ One Teach, One Facilitate
- ☐ One Teach, One Assess
- ☐ One Teach, One Take Data (specify data to be collected)
- ☐ One Teach, One Support
- ☐ One Teach, One Handle Materials
- ☐ Two Facilitate (whole group)
- ☐ Turn Taking

Reproducible

Level 1 Lesson Planner – Page 2

Role of Teacher 1 (include time switch and materials)	Roles of Teacher 2 (include time switch and materials)

Maximizing Co-Planning Time

Here are ten tips for advancing your co-planning time:

1. Notify each other in advance of planning. List the essential understandings to be taught, key concepts and points to discuss.

2. Exchange teaching materials before you meet.

3. Make an appointment.

4. Start and end on time.

5. Stick to work related issues, stay on task.

6. Save 5 minutes for social times at the end of the meeting, if needed.

7. Schedule your next collaborative meeting before you end.

8. Stick to a 15-20 minute time frame.

9. Keep a running log of your agenda and your meeting notes. Leave this log in a convenient place for both teachers to add to before the next meeting.

10. Speak from a "we" or "I" point of view and not from a "you" point of view.

Instructional Planning Ideas

Use Bloom's Taxonomy in your planning process. You may find, as I have, that referencing Bloom's verbs helps with the task of planning instruction around the higher order thinking areas.

Consider planning units instead of lessons. Use a learning styles unit planner for determining what visual, auditory, and kinesthetic activities will be used across the curriculum. **You don't need something kinesthetic for every single group every single day. However, you should have something kinesthetic each day, even if it is only in one group.** The challenge is to create kinesthetic opportunities that address the higher levels of Bloom's Taxonomy. Since most students with disabilities are kinesthetic learners, by incorporating hands-on and movement approaches, you increase the likelihood of students understanding and relating to the curriculum, which will lead to better outcomes for students.

The 3 Station Rotation planner that uses the Visual Auditory Kinesthetic or VAK method will help you structure a variety of activities. If you have the luxury of a paraprofessional assigned to one child in the classroom, think about whether the paraprofessional has to constantly stay at that child's side. That might be the case if the child is medically fragile, or has some other significant physical need. Otherwise, you may be able to use the paraprofessional in the independent group, which will help reduce the student/teacher ratio, and also prevents the assigned child from becoming enabled by the paraprofessional's constant presence. The paraprofessional can manage the independent group, ensuring that the kids get started and stay on task. Therefore, consider including plans for paraprofessionals embedded in your lesson plans.

Establish the patterns that work for you, get comfortable with them, try them out, get students used to moving desks and you'll find that very quickly, you will grow your program.

The Co-teaching Planner Level 2: Parallel, Mirror, Flip/Flop, Pre-teach with Enrich, and Flip/Flop with Specially Designed Instruction

Date	Teacher A role	Teacher B role	Accommodations, Modification and Specially Designed Instruction (IEP Goals to be addressed)

Bloom's Taxonomy Descriptors

The New Bloom's Taxonomy	Remembering	Understanding	Applying	Analyzing	Evaluating	Creating
Definitions	Exhibit memory of previously learned material by recalling facts, terms and basic concepts	Demonstrate understanding and ideas by organizing and comparing, translating and stating main ideas	Solve problems to new situations by applying acquired knowledge, facts, techniques and rules in a different way	Examine and break information into parts by identifying motives or causes. Make inferences and find evidence to support generalizations	Present and defend opinions by making judgments about information, validity of ideas or quality of work, based on a set of criteria	Compile information in different, new ways by combining elements in a new pattern or proposing an alternate solution
Descriptive Verbs	Fill in, recall, list, label, choose, memorize, repeat, recite, name, define, record, omit, select, spell	Paraphrase, restate, retell, summarize, report, discuss, review, explain, compare, contrast, translate, show, locate, rewrite, outline, infer, classify	Construct, apply, solve, interview, model, select, build, plan, organize, dramatize, manipulate, calculate, research, sequence, convert, illustrate, diagram, experiment with	Divide, conclude, classify, infer, inspect, dissect, analyze, categorize, survey, discover, deduce, differentiate, investigate, question, critique, appraise, test for	Rate, prioritize, justify, disprove, support opinion, award, rule on, explain, measure, defend, judge, decide, value, forecast	Compose, theorize, invent, adapt, originate, solve, improve, create, compile, hypothesize, synthesize, refine, transform, formulate

VAK Unit Planner with Bloom's Taxonomy

*Plan for the Highest Levels of Kinesthetic Learning When Using this Planner for Co-Teaching

Use this Unit Planner to determine where and how students will work in higher taxonomy areas

	Remembering	Understanding	Applying	Analyzing	Evaluating	Creating
Visual						
Auditory						
*Kinesthetic						

The VAK Planning Organizer for a Single Co-teaching Lesson (Three station rotation) - One Lesson, Level 2

	Teacher 1	Teacher 2	Independent Group, or Instructions for Paraprofessional
Visual			
Auditory			
Kinesthetic			

Four station rotation: mini lesson – lesson planner, Level 2

Station 1	Station 2	Station 3	Station 4
Timing:	Timing:	Timing:	Timing:
Directions:	Directions:	Directions	Directions:
Objective:	Objective:	Objective:	Objective:
Group:	Group:	Group:	Group:
Teacher's Role/ Independent Instructions:	Teacher's Role/ Independent Instructions:	Teacher's Role/ Independent Instructions:	Teacher's Role/ Independent Instructions:
Description of activity or lesson plan	Description of activity or lesson plan	Description of activity or lesson plan	Description of activity or lesson plan

Lesson Ideas

Example: Parallel Lessons with Learning Styles

Grades: Primary

Topic: Apples

Skill: Writing the letter A

Length of lesson: 30 minutes

Teacher A	Teacher B
1. Read big book and show: *How Apples Grow, by Betsy Maestro* *Students sit on squares in reading corner*	1. Slide show from computer on Lyman Orchards Farm: Apple Picking. Students sit on chairs around one table
2. Have students "pass the pointer" and point out letter A on each page	2. Students take turns identifying the letter A on each slide using a magnifier.
3. Students stand one at a time to make a letter A with their body	3. Students stand one at a time and make a letter A with their body
4. Students return to seats and practice letter A on dot paper	4. Students return to seats and practice writing the letter A on raised line paper.

Lesson Ideas

Example: 3 Station Rotation

Writing

Grade: Secondary

Topic: Writing, Introductory Paragraphs

Skills: CUTS writing, Grammar, and Editing

Length of Lesson: 45 minutes with 15-minute rotations

Teacher A	Teacher B	Independent Group
1. Teacher gives students a rubric for grading grammar.	1. Students are taught the CUTS (see next page) through verbal rehearsal.	1. Round robin, DOL Students assigned to work in pairs.
2. Teacher teaches students how to use the rubric.	2. Students then read a short passage put together by the teacher on: *Nutrasweet: Food or Poison* (Snopes.com and Manataka.org)	2. Each pair is given 4 envelopes with sentence strips. Each sentence needs corrections. There is a corresponding worksheet.
3. Teacher hands out example work samples and has students use a rubric to "grade" each sample for grammar.	3. Students react to the passage by using the CUTS FRAME (see page 127) in order to create an opening paragraph to express their opinion on the topic.	3. Students take turns being the "teacher" for each envelope. Student 1 points out correction, student 2 monitors answers. Corrections are made on the worksheet.

Step 1: State the strategy

Create an exciting question or did you know statement.

Use a connection (Text/Self, Text/Text, Text/World)

Try three facts

State what you will learn….And think of a snappy title

Step 2: Fill in the frame

Did you know

_____

_____

Text/Self/World Connection

_____

_____

Three facts

_____

_____

(Transition Word), what you will find is

_____

_____

Step 3: Use the frame to make sentences

Example from Frame: Food or Poison?

Did you know that a popular sweetener can be used as a poison?

On Sunday at Granny's house, this "poison" is in our food and drink.

We consume it in our iced tea. It kills carpenter ants. It makes a lot of money for a company.

Therefore, what you will find is many people advertise the use of NutraSweet™ even though some people claim it can be used as a poison.

Step 4: Clean up the sentences to make a paragraph

Example: Four station rotation: mini lesson – lesson planner – Grade level = generic. Level 2

Station 1 – REVIEW	Station 2 – RETEACH – Teacher A	Station 3 – PASS THE PROBLEM	Station 4 – RETEACH – Teacher B
Timing: 10 Minutes	*Timing:* 10 Minutes	*Timing:* 10 Minutes	*Timing:* 10 Minutes
Directions: Student Pairs Review using foldable study guide	*Directions:* Use data from CBA quiz to group students. Re-teach key concepts not mastered.	*Directions:* Practice math problems on white boards, 2 minutes per problem, self-correcting	*Directions:* Use data from CBA quiz to group students. Re-teach key concepts not mastered.
Objective: To review and memorize key vocabulary words	*Objective:* Data based interventions	*Objective:* Practice key concepts for test	*Objective:* Data based interventions
Group: Learning Partners (around room – not to sit as a group, sit in pairs)	*Group:* As determined by data (6 to 7 students)	*Group:* 6 to 7 students	*Group:* As determined by data (6 to 7 students)
Teacher's Role / Independent Instructions: Independent (Mrs. Jones to prepare group directions)	*Teacher's Role / Independent Instructions:* Mrs. Kunkel, to use Concrete Representation Abstract Approach to re-teach difficult concepts with manipulatives and tangible objects.	*Teacher's Role / Independent Instructions:* Independent (Mrs. Kunkel to prepare white boards using dry/wet erase markers, 2 minute egg timer)	*Teacher's Role / Independent Instructions:* Independent (Mrs. Jones to re-teach lessons 3 and 7 to emphasize key learning objectives.
Description of activity or lesson plan	Description of activity or lesson plan	Description of activity or lesson plan	Description of activity or lesson plan
Each pair will spend 2 minutes using rapid fire drill and their foldable to quiz each other for 2 minutes. Switch ever 2 minutes for 2 turns each..	Two groups will start with concrete examples using kinesthetic objects – manipulate objectives, then move to drawing pictures, then actual math problems. One group enrichment, one group focus on Representation and Abstract only.	One student will be the group manager and run the timer. Students given 2 minutes to complete self-correcting problems on white board. After two minutes, students erase and pass the board.	Review and re-teach lessons 3 and 7 using new examples, providing multiple practice opportunities opportunities to respond.

Finding the Time to Collaborate and Co-Plan

- **Hire substitutes.** Floating subs can be available on a rotating bi-weekly basis for collaboration and co-planning to occur. Subs can cover duties and non-instructional responsibilities. Two subs can be hired for a full day or a half-day.

- **Use of Interns.** Internships are becoming very popular on college campuses. Less than the cost of an aide, interns are generally seniors or post-graduates, fulfilling a college requirement before they begin student teaching. They can be available for coverage.

- **Volunteers.** Parents and school volunteers can help in two ways. They can either provide coverage, or act as a guest speaker. Arrange with a volunteer committee to have guest speakers once a month to come in and speak to the class about a career related to your current curriculum. Plan during these assemblies.

- **Technology.** To communicate, use the phone, fax, e-mail, Wiki spaces, online chat --or use a digital camera to have live e-conferences.

- **Paraprofessionals.** Use paraprofessionals to monitor a practice assignment for 15 minutes, while you meet in the back of the room to plan.

- **Schedule it.** Volunteer to be on the schedule committee in your school. Schedule planning time with your co-teacher. If your co-teacher has a duty such as study hall and you have concurrent planning time, agree to meet in study hall once a week.

- **Before or after school.** Meet before or after school once a week or once every other week, depending on your curriculum demands.

- **One teacher covers two classes.** A teacher in your department or team shows a film all students need to watch. You combine classes and alternate coverage during the film time to free one of you up to meet with another teacher.

- **Other professionals teach a class.** Guidance department meets with your class to cover their developmental guidance curriculum, or the school social worker does a lesson on problem solving. Plan during this time.

Finding Time Continued...

- **Professional Development Time.** Use some of your professional development time to create co-taught units.

- **Use Existing Planning Time.**

- **Rethink Faculty Meetings.** Are there some items that can be bulleted in a memo, freeing up 15 minutes for collaboration and co-planning to happen?

- **Summer Curriculum Writing.** Is this available for you to use to plan or collaborate to preset the year? Can you write a curriculum that will be based on two teachers in the classroom?

- **Release time.**

- **Lunch together?**

- **Found time.** Snow days, assemblies.

- **Student Teacher.** While the student teacher conducts a class, meet to plan.

Other Co-planning Tips

- Set up a scheduled planning time and stick to it.

- Map out the unit in advance on a calendar, then zoom in on specific co-taught lessons that need a lot of planning together (i.e. parallel or teaming).

- Vary your co-teaching configurations.

- Let the curriculum drive what co-teaching arrangements make sense for a given lesson.

- Schedule in your co-planning time before anything else...keep it sacred!

- Send each other your ideas in advance (notes, e-mail) so you are not starting from scratch.

- Try to plan about two weeks at a time. Review your plans weekly and make adjustments as necessary.

- **REMEMBER, if you don't co-plan...you can't co-teach.**

Advancing Your Use of Assessment/Data/Progress Monitoring Practices for Co–Teaching

DOMAIN 8

Domain VIII

Assessment/Data/Progress Monitoring

Co-teachers need to proactively plan their data / progress monitoring / assessment cycle. Advanced co-teachers meet to devise the best opportunities to ensure students can demonstrate competency for required materials. Decide how you and your partner will use assessment data to adjust instruction. Create a plan for how data will be collected, analyzed and reviewed on a regular basis.

- How will data be shared at team meetings?

- How will instructional protocols be followed to ensure fidelity of implementation?

- Co-teachers should ask questions such as, How will we grade students?

- Will both teachers have their names on report cards?

- Who will meet with parents for conferences? Who will manage grading system?

- Will students receive elaborated feedback from both teachers?

- How will data drive our flexible grouping decisions?

- What will we do if students are not making progress?

What are your current progress monitor processes?
Examine your practice with your co-teacher.

Assessment directions: Identify your co-teaching stages and create ideas and plans to advance your practices.

	Assessment/Data/Progress Monitoring	
	Developing systems of evaluation, adjusting standards and expectations, maintaining course integrity, using data to improve learning conditions and opportunities	
Stage 1 Level 1	• Two separate grading systems, separately maintained • Sometimes one grading system exclusively managed by general educator • Measures for evaluation are objective and solely examine the student's knowledge of content	Ideas for Advancing Practices in Assessment, Data, and Progress Monitoring:
Stage 2 Transition	• Teachers begin to explore alternate assessment ideas • Teachers begin to discuss how to effectively capture the students' progress • More performance measures of assessment are being used • Data is collected by one co-teacher	
Stage 3 Level 2	• Both teachers use a variety of options for progress monitoring • Both are comfortable with grading procedure for all students • There is specific monitoring & use of both objective and subjective standards for grading • Both teachers develop IEP goals and objectives and ways to integrate co-teaching activities • Both teachers assess all students and are familiar with student performance in all situations • Both teachers' names on the report card/assessment reporting • Collected data is analyzed, graphed and tracked for student progress. Data used to plan lessons, monitor progress • IEP data is collected, analyzed, discussed and reflected in flexible groups and class activities	

As co-teachers, how do you collect data? How do you use this data?
How will your roles and instruction be steered by data analysis?

Co-teaching and RTI
Tier 1 : Progress Monitoring

Progress Monitoring by Design

- Is a "thermometer" that allows for reliable, valid, cross-comparisons of data

- Determines whether students are benefiting from core instruction

- Develops interventions and groups for students who are not benefiting or making adequate progress

- Compares the efficacy of different forms of instruction / intervention (Level 2)

- Designs more effective, individualized interventions in a timely, responsive manner

- Establishes targets

  o Considers benchmarks set in general education and current student performance

  o Focuses on decision making to inform instruction and selection of intervention (type and intensity)

- Ensures IEP goals and specially designed instruction are embedded

- Uses multiple assessment measures

- Uses frequent probes

- Graphs and analyzes data

  o Level of progress

  o Rate of progress

Adapted from Ellen Cohn, with permission

Grading: Frequently Asked Questions

Are there any laws about grading students with disabilities?

Grading students is at the discretion of teachers based on district policies or guidelines. For children with IEPs, some court cases on this issue have identified two specific areas to consider: "In spite of" the child's disability, is the child otherwise qualified when given reasonable accommodations?; or 'because of' the child's disability, do you tend to grade in a certain way? If given reasonable accommodations, the child is achieving the general objectives of the course, then modified grading may not be necessary or appropriate. If you generally grade a certain way for all students with disabilities (ipse dixit), then you need to question whether this is an appropriate practice or not. If you modify grades based solely on the fact the student has an IEP, then this may be constructed as a discriminatory practice.

Cases to look at:

Southeastern v. Davis

Alexander v. Choate

Ottawa (IL) Office of Civil Rights (grading variances)

Grading decisions for a student with disabilities should be made at the IEP meeting, in advance of the child participating in the class.

What about putting "modified" on a report card?

The literature and many professionals suggest the following: it may be an acceptable practice to put modified on a report card as long as: 1. You use it for <u>any</u> student who receives any type of modification, not just a particular group of students…like students with disabilities; 2. It only goes on the report card and <u>not</u> on a transcript; 3. It never says "modified as per IEP" or anything that breaches confidentiality rules; 4. It is discussed at the IEP meeting. I suggest you develop guidelines around this area for the district to follow. Check these guidelines with your school and district-wide administration as well as counsel to make sure the policy is not discriminatory. Also, be careful how classes are identified on transcripts. "Special education math" is inappropriate for a transcript. "Essentials of math" is a good substitute.

Sample guideline: *"It should be the guideline of this school to employ differential standards for grading and course requirements. The general education classroom teacher is encouraged to modify the curriculum, instructional approaches, and grading practices for those identified as students with disabilities in the general classroom."*

Grading Continued...

Sample staff guideline: *"...The difference between a modification and an accommodation must be made clear to students and parents at the IEP meeting. A modification is a change to the curriculum objectives. Less content is expected to be mastered by the student. Generally, less written work is expected to be completed... Modifications must be asterisked on the report card for <u>any</u> student receiving a modification (even students without an IEP on file)... An accommodation is a strategy that allows a student access to the curriculum. They are aids certain students need to help them learn the same material the rest of the class is learning. Oral tests, additional time, repeated directions, and pre-teaching are some examples. Accommodations are explained to the parents, documented on the IEP or 504 plan, but do not have to be asterisked on the report card."*

Sample staff guideline: *"Students that receive modifications that change the objectives of the curriculum will be given a grade based on their IEP or 504 plan outcomes. The course will have a "7" at the end of the number. For example: Humanities, section 3, will be for students receiving regular credit and weight. Humanities 37 will be for students, who have been programmed (through an IEP) to receive alternate credit. This credit will be weighted differently, for class rank purposes."*

What will I say to other students or their parents?

Remember you are bound to keep certain information confidential. To be fair, you do not have to treat all students the same, you have to do what is right for each student.

What about honor roll and diplomas?

Ask yourself this... What is the honor roll... or a diploma for...? What does it represent? Who should be entitled? If a student completes what you ask them to do, and they make good grades, are they entitled? Did those students complete the same requirements? Some schools and states have varying degrees of diplomas that address this issue. These questions may be best answered through professional learning community research. Always seek advice on guidelines or policies with school counsel.

What about college or the employer?

Colleges have numerous ways for screening applicants. Students with disabilities can choose not to identify their disability in college or on the job. If they choose to identify, they are entitled to certain protections under section 504 and the Americans with Disabilities Act.

> Tip: Confer with school counsel before creating grading guidelines and/or policies for students with disabilities.

see **www.lrp.com** for more resources

Alternative Assessment Options

- Checklists
- Performance Based Learning Assessment
- Portfolio
- Audit
- Pass/Fail
- Contract Grade
- Multiple Grades
- Shared Grades
- Rubric Grading
- Strategy List
- Narrative
- Pre/post test (% increase based on selected skills)
- Conversation (talk to the student.. "Tell me what you know about-")

The purpose of assessment is to ensure the student demonstrates competency. **What is the best way for your students to demonstrate competency?** How can co-teachers multi-task during assessment? One co-teacher might orally quiz students one at a time for a one-minute probe, while the other teacher teaches. Consider all of your assessment options.

Relish a Recording

Usage: Maximizing inclusion

Can you record your tests on an MP3 player? Students can listen to the test in the classroom instead of being removed from class.

This strategy not only maximizes the inclusion of students with disabilities, it also fosters independence. Additionally, by using technology to assess student competency, it allows the co-teacher to dedicate more time to instruction.

PBLA's (Performance Based Learning Assessments)

These assessments can be easily modified by changing part of the task or by varying the point value of various items.

Assessment List for <u>ROMEO & JULIET</u> newspaper

Element	Point Value	Self Eval.	Teacher Eval.
1. The content of the article is accurate	20		
2. The article is written with a specific purpose in mind	10		
3. The article is well organized. It has a beginning, middle and an end	20		
4. The article is informative	10		
5. Spelling and punctuation are correct	15		
6. Grammar and sentence structure are okay	15		
7. The article is presented neatly	10		

Modification ideas

Element	Point Value	Self Eval.	Teacher Eval.
1. The content of the article is accurate	20		
2. The article is written with a specific purpose in mind	15		
3. The article is well organized. It has a beginning, middle and an end	15		
4. The article is informative	10		
5. Spelling and punctuation are correct	5		
6. Grammar and sentence structure are okay	15		
7. The article is presented neatly	10		
8. The student had a writing conference with draft 2	10		

For more information on PBLA's, please see "Teacher's Guide to Performance-Based Learning and Assessment" by Michael Hibbard et al. http://www.ascd.org/publications/books/196021.aspx

Students with IEPs can be graded based on an element rubric that correlates with the IEP specified goals. See page 142 for directions for using these rubrics.

Example Rubric Summaries
Alternative Grading: IEP Grading, Standards Based

Rubric Summary of <u>Language Arts</u>   Marking Period   1

<u>Written Expression:</u>

* paragraph writing	1	2	3	TA/SI
-indents to start a paragraph	1	2	3	TA/SI
-writes 4-5 related sentences per paragraph	1	2	3	TA/SI
-avoids repetition of words and ideas	1	2	3	TA/SI
-writes content relating to the topic of the writing prompt	1	2	3	TA/SI

<u>Literature:</u>

* answers 5 questions about the main idea of a story	1	2	3	TA/SI
* provides 2 important facts about each main character of a story	1	2	3	TA/SI
* describes the time and place of the story	1	2	3	TA/SI
* states the conclusion of a story	1	2	3	TA/SI
* predicts what might happen after the end of the story	1	2	3	TA/SI
* gives an opinion about the story, supported by three reasons	1	2	3	TA/SI
* makes a recommendation of the story/book to another reader by rating the material and explaining the reason for the rating	1	2	3	TA/SI

<u>Grammar, Spelling and Vocabulary</u>

* capitalizes the beginning word in sentences	1	2	3	TA/SI
* punctuates the end of sentences	1	2	3	TA/SI
* spells 10 – 15 Target words from <u>Wordskills</u>	1	2	3	TA/SI
* learns/reviews 10 – 15 Target word meanings	1	2	3	TA/SI
* practices vocabulary activities through:				
-synonyms exercises	1	2	3	TA/SI
-antonyms exercises	1	2	3	TA/SI
-multiple meanings	1	2	3	TA/SI
-related meanings	1	2	3	TA/SI
-meanings from context	1	2	3	TA/SI

IEP Key:

1 = 70 – 100%   2 = 70 – 50%   3 = below 50%
SI = self initiated   TA = with teacher assistance

Example Rubric Summaries
Alternative Grading- IEP Grading, Standards Based

Rubric Summary of __Geography__   Marking Period _____1_____

* uses an atlas index to locate information	1	2	3	TA/SI
* identifies place names	1	2	3	TA/SI
* transfers place names to a blank map	1	2	3	TA/SI
* learns basic cultures of countries by locating facts in the textbook	1	2	3	TA/SI
* writes one piece of information about religion and politics for that culture	1	2	3	TA/SI
* writes a description of family life, including three facts	1	2	3	TA/SI
* does one oral presentation and/or project per cultural study as modified by the teacher	1	2	3	TA/SI
* completes mini-project as modified by teacher	1	2	3	TA/SI
* participates in group work as directed by teacher	1	2	3	TA/SI
* keeps geography dictionary organized in her notebook	1	2	3	TA/SI

IEP Key:

1 = 70 – 100%   2 = 70 – 50%   3 = below 50%
SI = self initiated   TA = with teacher assistance

Rubric Summary of __Math__   Marking Period 1__

* demonstrates accuracy using the calculator for math problem solving	1	2	3	TA/SI
* demonstrates accuracy in whole number operations (+, -, x, ÷)	1	2	3	TA/SI
* shows knowledge of fractions using visuals and/or manipulatives	1	2	3	TA/SI
* shows ability to write decimal amounts from whole number operations (+, -, x, ÷)	1	2	3	TA/SI
* understands 2-place decimal value of money by fraction counting and/or fraction amounts	1	2	3	TA/SI
* demonstrates ability to solve 1-step problems by explaining solution	1	2	3	TA/SI
* demonstrates knowledge of measurement (clock, ruler, liquid, dry)	1	2	3	TA/SI
* shows ability to count money to $1, $5, $10, $25, $50, $75, $100	1	2	3	TA/SI
* can make change to $10, $20, $50, $70, $100	1	2	3	TA/SI
* given two products can make the best consumer choice and explain why	1	2	3	TA/SI
* budgets money: given a certain total for shopping, paying bills and planning a trip or vacation	1	2	3	TA/SI
* can figure food costs and unit prices through computation and problem solving	1	2	3	TA/SI

IEP Key

1 = 70 – 100%   2 = 70 – 50%   3 = below 50%
SI = self initiated   TA = with teacher assistance

The rubrics can be used to determine the progress monitoring data needed for an IEP. You may also use these rubrics to determine report card grades.

To use the rubrics for IEP progress monitoring, rate each element based on the key. First, develop the key to correlate with IEP goals for mastery. Example: if 80% mastery, then your 1 is based on that percentage.

To use the rubrics for grading, mark each element accordingly. Take a numerical average of each element to calculate a grade. For example: add up all of the 1's, 2's, and 3's. Divide by the number of elements being assessed to calculate a numerical "average." So if your total of 1's, 2's and 3's is "20" and you have twelve elements (as on page 141) the average is 1.7. On a pre-determined scale, a 1.7 might be equivalent to a B$^+$ for the report card.

Throughout the book, we have covered all eight components of the co-teaching rubric:

- Communication skills
- Physical arrangements
- Instructional presentation
- Classroom management
- Curriculum familiarity and differentiation of instruction
- IEP goals, modifications and embedded specially designed instruction
- Instructional planning
- Assessment/Data/Progress monitoring practices

When implementing these eight practices, it's important to remember that it's a personalized process. You and your co-teacher will make professional decisions about how to implement change because co-teaching, at its core, is two people functioning as one unit.

Continually revisit the co-teaching rubric and make plans with your co-teacher for strengthening your practice. Your best results will spring from on-going conversation, collaborative discussion, reflection of practice and the ability to adjust instruction on a regular basis. Students will benefit from your ability to unify your instructional expertise. Enjoy!

Visit my website for information on current co-teaching research
www.KunkelConsultingServices.com

Co-Teaching Resources

Frequently Asked Questions (FAQ) - Use these questions during your Professional Learning Community Conversations

- How do you find/create time to co-plan and prepare differentiated lessons?

- How do you pace the content when you have students of varying levels?

- Who deals with student discipline?

- How do you keep higher-achieving students engaged?

- How do you provide specially designed instruction to the students with disabilities while maintaining the integrity of the standards of the curriculum?

- What role does each teacher have in the room?

- Who is in charge of the co-taught classroom?

- Who is responsible for grading and assessment?

- Who communicates with parents?

- What do you tell students about having two teachers in the classroom?

- Who is in charge of making modifications and accommodations?

- How do you avoid the "good" student from doing all of the work in cooperative learning groups?

- How will rigor affect co-teaching?

- What is the best ratio of students with disabilities to students without disabilities?

- Are leveled classes (homogeneous groups) better for co-teaching?

- How important is it for co-teachers to work together for more than one year?

- What do you do if someone isn't working with you or pulling his/her own weight in terms of co-teaching?

- If general education responsibilities are shared, then are special education responsibilities shared as well?

- What do we do if co-teaching is not working for the adults (co-teachers –not the students)?

- What are some tips for raising test scores?

- How do we monitor progress?

- What are some suggestions for celebrating successes with the co-teaching class?

Select FAQ Answers From Teachers Across the United States

How do you find the time to plan?

- Decide on station topics and then be responsible for your own topics (limit amount of planning time you need by using station options)

- Use special times to plan

- Schedule a common time (in advance of the year starting)

- Co-teach on a 4 out of 5 day schedule and use the "off time" to plan

- Set aside "sacred" time, and then do! (weekly)

- Use a notebook to write back and forth to each other (leave it in the classroom)

- Tweet, blog, on-line chat, email…

- Use a building sub (who has a plan period) to cover during mundane tasks (watching a movie, silent reading) while teachers plan right outside classroom door

How do you use a paraprofessional during the co-teaching process?

- Have the paraprofessional facilitate one of the independent stations (and NOT follow any students with disabilities)

- Paraprofessional provides practice, drill, correction during a station

- Collect data: checklists, tally, frequency counts, fluency count, time on task…

- Include the paraprofessional during planning, provide them with a copy of the plans and the IEP goals being focused on during the lesson.

How do we monitor IEP goals in the general education classroom?

- Make a mini-list of goals and staple them into plan books

- Track/ take data on goals every two weeks, making a tracking schedule

- Use alternative groups to gain data every two weeks

- Keep anecdotal records on sticky notes and place them into the plan book

- Use data systems to track information and interventions
  (see: www.chartdog.com or www.easycbm.com)

Selected Bibliography

For additional copies of this text, or for Sonya Kunkel's newest books on co-teaching and other teaching strategies, please see www.KunkelConsultingServices.com

Co-Teaching Text

Benninghof, Anne M., *Co-Teaching That Works*, Jossey-Bass, San Francisco, CA 2012

Friend, Marilyn and Lynne Cook. *Interactions: Collaboration skills for school professionals, 4th ed.* Boston, ME: Allyn and Bacon, 2003.

Kunkel, Sonya Heineman, *Advancing your Co-Teaching Practices to Raise Student Achievement: a Value Added Instructional Intervention,* Kunkel Consulting Services, **www.kunkelconsultingservices.com**, 2011

Murawski, Wendy W., *Collaborative Teaching in Secondary Schools, Making the Co-teaching Marriage Work!,* Corwin Publications: A Sage Company, California, 2009

Reeves, Douglas B., *Leading Change in Your School: How to Conquer Myths, Build Commitment and Get Results,* ASCD, Alexandria, VA, 2009

Robb Laura, et. al., *Reader's Handbook, A Student's Guide for Reading and Learning*, Great Source, Wilmington, MA

Villa, Richard A. et al. *A Guide to co-teaching: Practical tips for facilitating student learning.* Thousand Oaks, CA: Corwin Press, 2004.

Walther-Thomas, Chriss, Lori Korinek, Virginia L. McLaughlin, Brenda Toler Williams, *Collaboration for Inclusive Education, Developing Successful Programs*, Allyn and Bacon, Boston, 2000.

Teaching and Learning Tools Text

Boyles, Nancy N., *That's a GREAT Answer! Teaching Literature Response to K-3, ELL and Struggling Readers,* Maupin House, Gainesville, FL, 2007

Byrd, Daphne, Polly Westfall, *Guided Reading Coaching Tool, 1-6,* Crystal Springs Books, NH, 2009

Diller, Debbie, *Literacy Work Stations,* Stenhouse Publications, Portland, Maine, 2003

Frei, Shelly, Teaching Mathematics Today, Shell Education, Huntington Beach, CA, 2007

Kartchner Clark, Sarah, *Writing Strategies for Social Studies,* Shell Education, Huntington Beach, CA, 2007

Kunkel, Sonya Heineman, and Margaret Rae MacDonald, Ph.D. *The Path to Positive Classroom Management,* Kunkel Consulting Services, **www.kunkelconsultingservices.com**, 2012

Kunkel, Sonya Heineman *Simple and Powerful Teaching and Learning Strategies for Embedding Specially Designed Instruction in General Classrooms,"* Kunkel Consulting Services, **www.kunkelconsultingservices.com**, 2012

Macceca, Stephanie, *Reading Strategies for Science,* Shell Education, Huntington Beach, CA, 2007

McAndrews, Stephanie, *Diagnostic Literacy Assessments and Instructional Strategies, A Literacy Specialist's Resource,* International Reading Association, Newark, DE, 2008

Silver, Harvey F., et. al., *So Each May Learn: Integrated Learning Styles and Multiple Intelligences,* ASCD, Alexandria, VA, 2000

Silver, Harvey F., et al, Tools *for Promoting Active, In-Depth Learning,* The Thoughtful Education Press, 2001

Sliva, Julie A., *Teaching Inclusive Mathematics to Special Learners, K-6,* Corwin Press, Thousand Oaks, CA, 2004

Tilton, Linda, *The Teacher's Toolbox for Differentiating Instruction, 700 Strategies, Tips, Tools and Techniques,* Covington Cove Publications, Shorewood, MN, 2005

Tomlinson, Carol Ann, Caroline Cunningham Eidson, *Differentiation in Practice: A Resource Guide For Differentiating Curriculum, Grades 5-9,* ASCD, Alexandria, VA, 2003

Vaughn, Sharon, Sylvia Linan-Thompson, *Research-Based Methods of Reading Instruction Grades K-3,* ASCD, Alexandria, VA, 2004

Videos

Friend, Marilyn, *The Power Of 2*, Forum on Education Production: second edition, 1996.

Beninghof, Anne, *Co-Teaching In Inclusive Classrooms, Part I (K-6)*, BER, Bellevue, WA, **www.ber.org**

Beninghof, Anne, *Co-Teaching In Inclusive Classrooms, Part I (K-6)*, BER, Bellevue, WA, **www.ber.org**

Kunkel, Sonya Heineman, *Practical Classroom Strategies for Making Inclusion Work, Grades 6-12,* BER, **www.ber.org** 2009

Kunkel, Sonya Heineman, *Using Co-teaching to Increase the Learning of All Students, Part I: Easy to Implement Strategies,* BER, Bellevue, WA, **www.ber.org**

Kunkel, Sonya Heineman, Using *Co-teaching to Increase the Learning of All Students, Part II: Strategies that Maximize the Instructional Impact of Inclusion Classrooms,* BER, Bellevue, WA **www.ber.org**

Audio

Beninghof, Anne, *Co-Teaching That Works***,** Effective Strategies for Working Together in Today's Inclusive Classrooms (Grades 1-12), BER, **www.ber.org**

Kunkel, Sonya Heineman, *Practical Classroom Strategies for Making Inclusion Work, (Grades 6-12)*, BER, Bellevue, WA, **www.ber.org**

Websites

Friend, Marilyn, "The co-teaching connection", **http://www.marilynfriend.com/index.htm**

Hibbard, Michael, et al., *Teacher's Guide to Performance-Based Learning and Assessment,* 1996, (publisher: ASCD) **http://www.ascd.org/publications/books/196021.aspx**

Huggins, Marie, Jennifer Huyghe, and Elizabeth Iljkoski, "Co-Teaching 101: Lessons from the Trenches", **http://www.cec.sped.org/**

"Keys to Effective Co-teaching Models: Needs Assessment and Program Planning", Developed for the Arkansas Department of Education, Co-teaching Professional Development Team, **University of Central Florida, http://arksped.k12.ar.us/documents/co_teaching/building_leadership_team_module.pdf**

Lawton, Millicent. "Co-teaching: Are two heads better than one in an Inclusion classroom? " *Harvard Education Letter* March/April 1999. 29 Aug. 2006 **http://www.edletter.org/past/issues/1999-ma/coteaching.shtml**

Marston, Natalie. "6 Steps to successful co-teaching." National Education Association. 2006. 29 Aug. 2006 **http://www.nea.org/teachexperience/spedk031113.html**

Tools for Teaching, **www.FredJones.com**

A Few Response to Intervention Web Sites:

www.interventioncentral.com - A good starting point (many links)

www.fcrr.org - Florida Center for Reading Research

www.chartdog.com – Graphing and Charting

www.easycbm.com - Progress Monitoring Assessment Tools Reading and Mathematics

www.rti4success.org - Another good starting point

**For additional materials, including the new co-teaching APP
for android smart phones, as well as resources, coaching
or professional development opportunities,
contact Sonya Heineman Kunkel.
www.KunkelConsultingServices.com**

Index

Notes Page

Made in the USA
San Bernardino, CA
27 April 2016